CODING WITH MINECRAFT®

CODING WITH MINECRAFT®

BUILD TALLER, FARM FASTER, MINE DEEPER, AND AUTOMATE THE BORING STUFF

BY AL SWEIGART

no starch press

San Francisco

CODING WITH MINECRAFT. Copyright © 2018 by Al Sweigart.

Printed in USA

Second printing

22 21 20 19 18   2 3 4 5 6 7 8 9

ISBN-10: 1-59327-853-5
ISBN-13: 978-1-59327-853-3

Publisher: William Pollock
Production Editor: Laurel Chun
Cover Illustration: Josh Ellingson
Developmental Editor: Jan Cash
Technical Reviewer: Daniel Ratcliffe
Copyeditor: Anne Marie Walker
Compositor: Meg Sneeringer
Proofreader: Shannon Waite

For information on distribution, translations, or bulk sales, please contact No Starch Press, Inc. directly:

No Starch Press, Inc.
245 8th Street, San Francisco, CA 94103
phone: 1.415.863.9900; info@nostarch.com
www.nostarch.com

Library of Congress Cataloging-in-Publication Data

Names: Sweigart, Al, author.
Title: Coding with Minecraft: build taller, farm faster, mine deeper,
   and automate the boring stuff / Al Sweigart.
Description: San Francisco : No Starch Press, Inc., [2018] | Includes
   index.
Identifiers: LCCN 2017046330 (print) | LCCN 2017058488 (ebook) | ISBN
   9781593278540 (ebook) | ISBN 1593278543 (ebook) | ISBN 9781593278533
   (pbk.) | ISBN 1593278535 (pbk.).
Subjects: LCSH: Minecraft (Game) | Lua (Computer program language) | Computer
   programming.
Classification: LCC GV1469.35.M535 (ebook) | LCC GV1469.35.M535 S94 2018
   (print) | DDC 794.8--dc23
LC record available at https://lccn.loc.gov/2017046330

To Daniel Ratcliffe, the ComputerCraft creator,
and Seymour Papert, the turtle creator

ABOUT THE AUTHOR

Al Sweigart is a professional software developer who teaches programming to kids and adults. Sweigart has written several bestselling programming books for beginners, including *Automate the Boring Stuff with Python, Invent Your Own Computer Games with Python,* and *Cracking Codes with Python* (all from No Starch Press). His books are freely available under a Creative Commons license at *https:// inventwithpython.com/*.

ABOUT THE TECHNICAL REVIEWER

Daniel Ratcliffe is a game developer from Cambridge, England. He created the ComputerCraft mod for Minecraft in 2011 and has been making games since 2002. You can read about his latest projects on Twitter, @DanTwoHundred. His other interests include *Star Trek,* cycling, and cats.

BRIEF CONTENTS

CONTENTS IN DETAIL

9
BUILDING A COBBLESTONE GENERATOR
99

10
MAKING A STONE BRICK FACTORY
113

11
CONSTRUCTING WALLS
127

ACKNOWLEDGMENTS

It's misleading to have just my name on the cover. This book wouldn't exist without the efforts of many people. I'd like to thank my publisher, Bill Pollock; my developmental editors, Jan Cash and Annie Choi; my production editor, Laurel Chun; my technical reviewer, Daniel Ratcliffe; my copyeditor, Anne Marie Walker; and all of the staff at No Starch Press. I'd also like to thank Josh Ellingson for a great cover illustration.

Thanks to Michelle and Doug Rapp for introducing me to Minecraft and punching trees.

INTRODUCTION

"Just three more diamonds, and then I'll stop," I remember telling myself while playing Minecraft. I needed the diamonds for a new pickaxe. I needed the pickaxe to mine more obsidian. I needed the obsidian to make a Nether portal. I needed to go to the Nether to pick up lava. And I needed the lava for . . . what did I need the lava for again? Oh, right. I was sculpting a giant phoenix statue in the side of a mountain, and I wanted to make lava pour out from its eyes and beak. Two hours later, I was still playing, unable to pry myself away from the task at hand.

Minecraft is an addictive game. It has sold over 107 million copies, making it the second most popular video game of all time, beaten only by Tetris. It's an open-ended, creative platform for gathering resources and building whatever you can imagine. You can build castles to protect against zombie hordes, plant crops and tend to animals, or team up with friends to build massive works of art. Minecraft appeals to a diverse set of people: children, teenagers, and even adults love playing it.

In this book, you'll use the ComputerCraft mod (also known as CC) to turn your addiction to building into an addiction to coding. But what exactly is ComputerCraft—or a mod, for that matter?

WHAT ARE MINECRAFT MODS?

Minecraft by itself, called *vanilla Minecraft*, is just the beginning. Minecraft can be modified and extended by third-party software called *mods* (short for *modifications*) to provide additional features such as blocks, environments, items, monsters, and even worlds that are not included with the vanilla version of the game. Due to its popularity, Minecraft has attracted one of the largest modding communities of any video game.

These fan-made mods are free to download. Some mods add space exploration and rockets. Others add sorcery and spells. You can even find Minecraft mods for creating your own dinosaur zoos, high-speed train networks, and bee-breeding apiaries. In this book, we'll use the ComputerCraft mod to learn how to program.

WHAT IS COMPUTERCRAFT?

ComputerCraft is a Minecraft mod that adds programmable turtles to Minecraft. These turtles can do almost anything the player can do: dig mines, chop down trees, construct buildings, craft items, plant seeds, milk cows, bake cakes, and more (see Figure 1). An army of these box-shaped turtles can automatically perform all the time-intensive chores the player usually must do manually.

Figure 1: Turtles chopping trees (left) and mining (right)

The catch is that you have to learn to program first. These turtles understand code written in Lua (*moon* in Portuguese), which is a programming language used by professional software developers in fields such as embedded computing systems and video game development. The interpreter software that runs Lua scripts is just 100KB, which means that it can be easily embedded inside other pieces of software, such as a Minecraft mod. Lua is often used within video game code—for example, in *World of Warcraft, Dark Souls, Portal 2, Factorio,* and many others.

Although Lua is simpler than other programming languages, it's still fast and powerful. These qualities work in your favor. Lua's simplicity makes it a good language to start with if you have no programming experience.

HOW TO USE THIS BOOK

You'll need a purchased copy of Minecraft for Windows or macOS, the free ComputerCraft mod, and the free ATLauncher software to use this book. See Chapter 1 for all download and installation instructions.

When typing the source code from this book, do not type the line numbers at the start of each line. For example, if you saw the following line of code, you would not need to type the 9. on the left side or the one space immediately following it:

```
9. print('What is your name?')
```

You'd enter only this:

```
print('What is your name?')
```

The numbers are there just so this book can refer to specific lines in the program. They are not part of the actual program's source code.

Sometimes you'll also see an unnumbered *...snip...* line in the code. This indicates that some code has been omitted for brevity. The *...snip...* is not part of the code itself.

WHAT'S IN THIS BOOK?

After the first few chapters, which cover basic programming concepts, each chapter in this book focuses on how to write a program your turtle can run to help you survive and thrive in Minecraft. You'll also find bonus activities that help you test your programming skills.

Here's what you'll find in each chapter:

- **Chapter 1: Getting Started with ComputerCraft** helps you install and set up Minecraft and the ComputerCraft mod so you can start programming.
- **Chapter 2: Programming Basics** introduces you to basic programming concepts and the interactive shell.
- **Chapter 3: Talking to Your Turtle** introduces the file editor, which you'll use to write your first program.
- **Chapter 4: Programming Turtles to Dance** shows you how to write a program to move the turtles around the Minecraft world.
- **Chapter 5: Making a Better Dancer** adds on to the previous chapter's dancing program with some new programming instructions.

- **Chapter 6: Programming a Robot Lumberjack** features a program to make a turtle chop down a single tree and collect its wood.
- **Chapter 7: Creating Modules to Reuse Your Code** teaches you how to write code once and share it with multiple programs.
- **Chapter 8: Running an Automated Tree Farm** extends the program from Chapter 6 to create a fully automated tree farm so your turtles can harvest wood from multiple trees.
- **Chapter 9: Building a Cobblestone Generator** features a program for mining unlimited amounts of cobblestone, which the turtles will use as building material for Chapters 10 through 13.
- **Chapter 10: Making a Stone Brick Factory** features a program to turn the cobblestone from Chapter 9 into stone bricks.
- **Chapter 11: Constructing Walls** includes a program that uses stone bricks to build walls.
- **Chapter 12: Constructing Rooms** contains a program that lets you join walls together to build rooms.
- **Chapter 13: Constructing Floors** features a program to build floors and ceilings for your rooms.
- **Chapter 14: Programming a Robotic Farm** features a program to make turtles plant and harvest different kinds of crops so you can keep yourself fed.
- **Chapter 15: Programming a Staircase Miner** features a program that digs stairs deep into the ground to mine ore and other valuable blocks.
- The **Function Reference** lists and explains how to use all the functions in this book.
- The **Name ID Reference** lists commonly used Minecraft blocks and items along with their name IDs, which you'll use to identify block types and other items in your programs.

GETTING HELP

Minecraft famously lacks a tutorial for new players. It doesn't have an instruction manual or even a help menu. Minecraft forces you to be responsible for your own education. You'll need to do online research, form questions, find answers, and sometimes just do some plain old experimentation. Minecraft cultivates a *growth mindset* in players. Even after falling into lava or having their base blown up by a creeper, players come back determined to learn how to overcome these problems.

However, this book is about the ComputerCraft mod, not the basics of playing Minecraft. To use this book, you should already know how to do the following in Minecraft:

- Mine for ore, stone, coal, wood, and other blocks
- Craft a workbench and tools such as axes, shovels, torches, and pickaxes

- Craft a furnace, fuel it, and then smelt ore blocks or cook meat in it
- Craft stairs, ladders, chests, doors, fences, and other parts you'll use for buildings
- Plant seeds and farm food

If you don't know how to do all of these things, don't worry. You can teach yourself by searching online. Go to the search engine of your choice and enter the word *minecraft* along with what you want to learn. For example, you could use the search terms *minecraft smelt ore*, *minecraft bake cake*, or even just *minecraft basic tutorial* to find the information you need. You can also search for Minecraft video tutorials on websites such as *https://www.youtube .com/* by using the same search terms you would use in a search engine.

As I mentioned previously, because ComputerCraft isn't made by the same people as Minecraft, most Minecraft websites won't have information about CC. You can learn about CC from the ComputerCraft Wiki at *http://www.computercraft.info/wiki/*. If you have questions specific to CC, you can sign up for a free account on the ComputerCraft forums at *http:// www.computercraft.info/forums2/*. If you have additional questions about the programs in this book, you can post those to the community at *https:// www.reddit.com/r/turtleappstore/*.

ONLINE RESOURCES

You can download all the programs in this book directly from inside the Minecraft game (see "Sharing and Downloading Programs Online" on page 42 for instructions). And, although Minecraft doesn't support copying and pasting text from outside the game, all the code and resources for this book are available for reference on its companion website, *https://www .nostarch.com/codingwithminecraft/*. There, you can also download the code for the bonus activities if you get stuck and want to check out the solutions! You'll also find links to the installation files (see Chapter 1 for detailed installation instructions). If you want to explore other programs or share your code, you can do so through *https://turtleappstore.com/*, which is a free website for ComputerCraft scripts (see "turtleappstore.com" on page 44 for details).

WHAT YOU LEARNED

Minecraft is a gaming phenomenon that can be played in many ways and appeals to a diverse crowd of players. In this book, you'll learn how to build more in less time using ComputerCraft, a mod that lets you program turtles in the Lua programming language. By learning to program with Lua and CC, you can automate many jobs you would otherwise have to do by yourself, including mining, farming, building, and crafting.

Using Minecraft and ComputerCraft, you'll solve problems independently and learn basic computer programming skills along the way.

Let's begin!

1

GETTING STARTED WITH COMPUTERCRAFT

Before you can start programming robotic turtles to do your bidding, you'll need to install and set up Minecraft and the ComputerCraft mod. Fortunately, the free ATLauncher software makes this process painless. In this chapter, I'll show you how to obtain Minecraft and the ComputerCraft mod, and then I'll walk you through all the configuration steps you'll need to do before you start programming.

INSTALLING MINECRAFT, ATLAUNCHER, AND COMPUTERCRAFT

Configuring Minecraft's mods used to be tricky because it involved a series of complicated steps. However, you can now use the ATLauncher software to load mods into Minecraft more easily. Because Minecraft, ATLauncher, and

ComputerCraft are created by different groups, you'll need to download and install each program separately. All three are available for the Windows, macOS, and Ubuntu operating systems, but the ComputerCraft mod isn't available for Minecraft on mobile, Xbox, or PlayStation platforms.

Mods only work for Minecraft's Java Edition, which is also called the Windows version of Minecraft. The Windows 10 version of Minecraft doesn't support mods, although it supports a new form of mods called *add-ons*. But don't worry! We'll be using software called ATLauncher to download and install the correct version of Minecraft.

BUYING MINECRAFT ONLINE

Although ATLauncher and ComputerCraft are free, Minecraft is sold by Mojang (now owned by Microsoft). You can buy it online at *https://www .minecraft.net/* after you create a free Mojang account. When you complete this purchase, don't download Minecraft from this site. Instead, you'll use the ATLauncher software to download and install Minecraft to your computer. (If you already have Minecraft installed, you should still follow the instructions to install Minecraft with ATLauncher.)

NOTE *Keep your Mojang account password safe and secret. Don't share it with friends or people who claim to be Mojang employees. Use it only to log into the ATLauncher software or the* https://www.minecraft.net/ *website and no other sites. If you think someone else might be logging into your account, change your password immediately.*

DOWNLOADING AND INSTALLING ATLAUNCHER

The ATLauncher software makes it easy to add mods to Minecraft. Figure 1-1 shows how you can download it for free at *https://www.atlauncher.com/*. Click the **Downloads** link at the top of the page to find the installation help video. Follow the steps in the video to download and install ATLauncher. The video is also available on YouTube at *https://youtu.be/gTf7rRCwMcI/*.

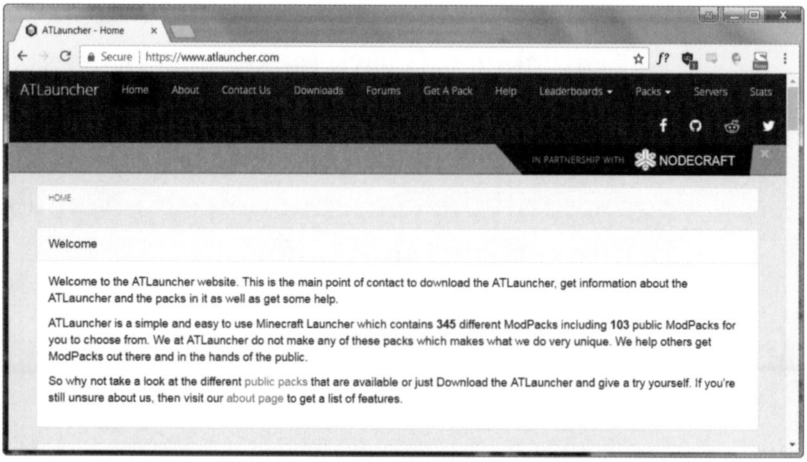

Figure 1-1: The ATLauncher website, where you can download the software

After installing ATLauncher, run it and click the **Accounts** tab on the right side. Fill in your Mojang account's username and password. You can select **Remember password** so you don't have to enter this information each time you run Minecraft.

To connect to a Minecraft server, you must install the same mods (and versions of each mod) as the server. Because so many mod combinations are possible, fans have created *modpacks* that consist of a standardized set of mods. We'll download a "vanilla" modpack (that is, a modpack with very few mods) now, and we'll add the ComputerCraft mod next. Click **Packs** and find the Vanilla Minecraft modpack. You'll add ComputerCraft to this version of Minecraft.

Click the **New Instance** button for the Vanilla Minecraft modpack. An *instance* is an installation of a particular modpack on your computer. In the window that appears, name the instance something like **CC Minecraft**. *Be sure to select **1.8.9 (Minecraft 1.8.9)** for the version to install because this is currently the latest version that ComputerCraft supports.* Leave Enable User Lock unchecked. Enabling the user lock means that only the Windows, macOS, or Linux user you are logged in as will be able to access this instance.

NOTE *Future versions of ComputerCraft may be compatible with newer versions of Minecraft. In this case, up-to-date installation instructions will become available at* https://www .nostarch.com/codingwithminecraft/.

In the Select Mods to Install window that appears, select only the box next to **Minecraft Forge (Recommended)** and then click **Install**. The Minecraft Forge mod is required for ComputerCraft.

USING A MOD ON A SERVER

When you first play Minecraft, I recommend playing in Singleplayer mode. But if you want to connect to a public multiplayer server, your instance needs to have the same mods as the server. Most public servers won't have just the ComputerCraft mod installed, so you'll need to install a modpack instance that isn't Vanilla Minecraft from the Packs tab instead. Popular modpacks that include ComputerCraft are Resonant Rise, Sky Factory 2, Space Astronomy, The Golden Cobblestone, and Yogscast Complete. (My favorite is Resonant Rise.) You can also browse the list of modpacks on ATLauncher's Packs tab and click the **View Mods** button to see whether ComputerCraft is included. If you use one of these modpacks, you can skip the instructions in "Downloading and Installing ComputerCraft" on page 4 because the correct version of ComputerCraft and Minecraft will automatically be installed with the pack. Modpacks have version numbers, so when you play on public servers, you'll need to install the same version of the modpack that the server uses.

To find public servers for these modpacks, do a web search for *<modpack name> public servers* or go to *https://www.atlauncher.com/* and click the **Servers** link at the top.

When the installation is finished, you can find your instance of Minecraft by selecting the **Instances** tab on the right side of the ATLauncher window. This instance is for Vanilla Minecraft, so you'll have to manually download and install ComputerCraft.

DOWNLOADING AND INSTALLING COMPUTERCRAFT

This section tells you how to download and install the ComputerCraft mod. There is also a video that shows how to install ComputerCraft at *https:// youtu.be/g4Zs2JY1vi8/*. You can download the ComputerCraft mod at *http:// www.computercraft.info/download/*. Click the **Download ComputerCraft 1.79 (for Minecraft 1.8.9)** link to download the file *ComputerCraft1.79.jar*. This file is also available at *https://www.nostarch.com/codingwithminecraft/*.

I like to keep this file in ATLauncher's folder so that it's easy to find. On ATLauncher's Instances tab, click the **Edit Mods** button next to your Vanilla Minecraft instance. You'll see the Editing Mods for CC Minecraft window, as shown in Figure 1-2, which currently has only the Minecraft Forge (Recommended) mod installed and enabled.

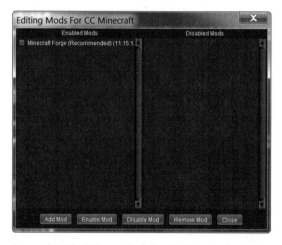

Figure 1-2: The Editing Mods for CC Minecraft window

Click the **Add Mod** button, and in the window that appears, click the **Select** button and find the *ComputerCraft1.79.jar* file you downloaded. Next to Type of Mod, select **Inside Minecraft.jar** from the drop-down menu. Then click the **Add** button.

The *ComputerCraft1.79.jar* file will appear on the right side under Disabled Mods. This mod is now installed to your Minecraft instance, but you must enable it to use it. Select the checkbox next to **ComputerCraft1.79 .jar**, and then click the **Enable Mod** button at the bottom of the window. The ComputerCraft mod will move to the left side of the window under Enabled Mods. Click the **Close** button to complete the process.

Return to the Instances tab, and click the **Play** button next to your Minecraft instance to launch the game. The first time you click **Play**, a window will appear telling you that an update is available, as shown in Figure 1-3. Click the **Don't Remind Me Again** button to refuse the update and hide this window in the future.

If you accidentally click Yes and update the instance, the ComputerCraft mod might not work correctly. You'll have to delete the instance and repeat all the instance and mod-adding steps again.

Figure 1-3: The Update Available window

CONFIGURING COMPUTERCRAFT

ComputerCraft has some configurable settings stored in a text file named *ComputerCraft.cfg*. In general, you don't need to modify this file, and this book assumes you're using the default configuration. Most public multiplayer Minecraft servers use the default configuration too. However, if you want to change CC's settings for any reason, you'll need to know where the configuration file is located.

You'll find this file on your computer under the same subfolders where you installed ATLauncher. On my Windows computer, I've installed ATLauncher in the *C:\ATLauncher* folder, so the configuration file is located in *C:\ATLauncher\Instances\CCMinecraft\config\ComputerCraft.cfg*. Open this file in a text editor, such as Notepad or TextMate. The settings are described in the file, and you can change them by entering new values after the equal signs (=).

RUNNING MINECRAFT

After you've run ATLauncher and clicked the **Play** button, Minecraft's main menu will appear, as shown in Figure 1-4.

Figure 1-4: Minecraft's main menu

Click the **Singleplayer** button, which should take you to a list of Minecraft worlds you've made. If this is the first time you're running Minecraft, you'll need to create a world.

CREATING A NEW WORLD

Minecraft does not have a standard set of levels. Rather, the game world is randomly generated and always provides you with a new, unknown area to explore. From the Singleplayer menu, click the **Create New World** button, and the Create New World menu will appear, as shown in Figure 1-5. Enter the name `My CC World` in the **World Name** text field. Then click the **Game Mode** button until it displays Game Mode: Survival. (You'll also be able to switch modes while playing the game.)

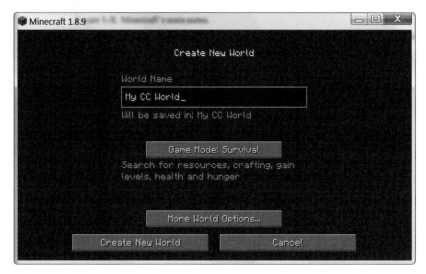

Figure 1-5: The Create New World menu

Click the **More World Options…** button, and then click the **Allow Cheats** button until it displays Allow Cheats: ON. Cheats will allow you to switch between the Survival and Creative game modes, which is explained next. To generate the new world, click the **Create New World** button.

MINECRAFT GAME MODE DIFFERENCES

Minecraft has three modes you can play in: Creative, Survival, and Hardcore.

In *Creative* mode, you can fly, don't need to eat, can't die, and will have an unlimited supply of all blocks. This mode is ideal if you just want to create structures out of Minecraft blocks, such as castles or giant artwork.

In *Survival* mode, things get real. You'll need to find food to prevent yourself from starving. The only blocks you get to build with are the ones you've mined yourself. You can't fly, and if you fall off a cliff, you'll take damage or even die. At night, monsters come out.

Because you set the Allow Cheats option to ON when you created the world, you'll be able to use the /gamemode command to switch between the Survival and Creative modes. To change the game mode, press the T key to open the chat window and enter **/gamemode creative** or **/gamemode survival**, as shown in Figure 1-6.

Figure 1-6: Entering the /gamemode creative command into the chat window

I think playing in Survival mode makes the game more challenging and fun. Resources are limited and you have to work for your blocks. Survival mode is also where ComputerCraft shines. By programming turtles to help you automate boring chores, you can keep yourself fed, safe, and well stocked while braving the elements.

Don't worry about dying in Survival mode. When you die, you'll drop the items that you were carrying and start back at your original spawn point, but you can keep playing.

Hardcore mode is similar to Survival mode, but you get one life and one life only. After dying, you must delete the game world. ComputerCraft also works in Hardcore mode, but I recommend sticking to Survival mode for now.

WHAT YOU LEARNED

You've now completed all the setup steps you need to use this book. You downloaded and installed Minecraft, ATLauncher, and the ComputerCraft mod. As mentioned earlier, ATLauncher and ComputerCraft are free. Minecraft is not.

Minecraft is so big and has so many mods that it took a bit of setup to get going. But now that you're ready to play, you're also ready to start learning to code, so let's write some code!

2

PROGRAMMING BASICS

In this chapter, we'll explore the basics of crafting Minecraft robots, or *turtles*. We'll create our first turtle and name it. Then we'll fuel it up and try out a few programming instructions! You'll also learn some basic programming concepts and how you can practice coding in Minecraft.

GETTING STARTED WITH TURTLES

The Logo programming language, created in the 1960s, introduced programmable turtles. In Logo, turtles were dots on the screen that you could program to move around and draw lines, creating amazing patterns. Using Logo, you could learn to program while creating art with your computer! Figure 2-1, made using a program from *Teach Your Kids to Code* by Bryson Payne (No Starch Press, 2015), shows an example of Logo-style art written in the Python programming language.

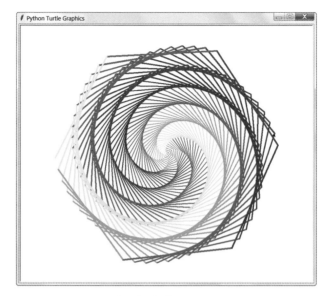

Figure 2-1: An example of colorful turtle art

ComputerCraft brings the same idea to the Minecraft world, where turtles are robots that can mine and craft according to programs *you* write. Figure 2-2 shows what these block-shaped turtle robots (also called *bots*) look like.

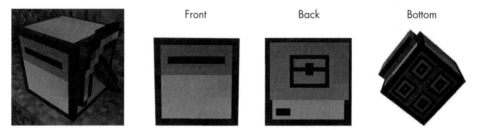

Figure 2-2: A turtle equipped with a pickaxe (left) and what turtles look like from different sides

These boxy bots may not look like much, but they have a lot of potential. Turtles can move in all directions. They can hover, survive underwater, carry items, and move through lava. Once you've mastered some programming skills, your turtles will carry out complex tasks at your command.

CRAFTING A MINING TURTLE

When you're in Creative mode, you can spawn a turtle just like any other item. You spawn a turtle by pressing E to open your inventory, clicking the compass tab, and then typing **turtle** to find all the different types of turtles, as shown in Figure 2-3. This book uses the gray *basic turtles* instead of the gold *advanced turtles*, but they work similarly.

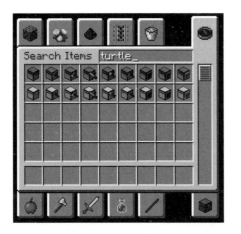

Figure 2-3: Spawning a turtle in Creative mode

NOTE   *To switch to Creative mode, press T or the / key to bring up the chat/command window; then enter /gamemode* **creative** *and press* ENTER. *To switch to Survival mode, press T or the / key and enter /gamemode* **survival**.

But we want to use turtles in Survival mode, where we'll need to craft turtles (along with everything else) from scratch. Here's how to do it.

1. **Craft a computer.** The turtle-crafting recipe requires a computer, so before we can craft a turtle, we must craft a computer using stone, redstone, and a glass pane. (If you don't know how to make stone or glass panes, or where to find redstone, open a web browser to a search engine site and enter "minecraft find redstone" or "minecraft craft glass pane.") To craft a computer, we'll follow the recipe in Figure 2-4.

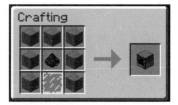

Figure 2-4: Crafting a computer with seven stone blocks, one redstone block, and one glass pane

2. **Use the computer to craft a turtle.** We won't bother placing the computer in the world because we won't be using it in this book. We just need it as a crafting item in the turtle recipe. We'll use the computer, some iron, and a chest to craft a basic turtle, as shown in the recipe in Figure 2-5.

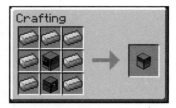

Figure 2-5: Crafting a turtle with seven iron blocks, one chest, and one computer

3. **Equip the turtle with tools!** So far, we just have a basic turtle. It can move around, but it can't mine, dig, or do much else until we give it a tool. We can equip turtles with diamond pickaxes, shovels, axes, hoes, or swords. These tools must be diamond tools *and* brand new. An iron tool or a diamond tool with wear and tear won't work. We can also equip turtles with crafting tables.

For our first turtle, let's use a diamond pickaxe to craft a mining turtle by following the recipe in Figure 2-6.

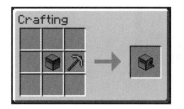

Figure 2-6: Crafting a mining turtle with one turtle and one diamond pickaxe

RUNNING PROGRAMS IN THE TURTLE GUI

To use the turtle, right-click to place it in the world, just as you would place any other block. Then, right-click the turtle to open its *graphical user interface (GUI)*, which is where you'll program the turtle and manage its inventory. Keep in mind that Minecraft isn't paused while you're looking at the GUI, so you need to be careful that monsters don't sneak up behind you while you're entering commands. Figure 2-7 shows what the turtle's GUI looks like.

Figure 2-7: The turtle's GUI

The GUI consists of your inventory, the turtle's inventory, and the *command shell*, which is where you'll write your programs and enter commands. (Oddly enough, the terms *shell* and *turtle* are just a coincidence.) You can store multiples of the same items in a single inventory slot to create a *stack* of items. For most items, you can stack up to 64 items in a single slot. Turtles have 16 inventory slots, and you can easily drag items between your inventory and the turtle's.

Turtles come preloaded with some programs, including label, dance, refuel, go, and lua. We should first name our turtle using the label program. In this book, I've named the turtles after four Italian Renaissance painters: Sofonisba, Lavinia, Artemisia, and Elisabetta. You can use these names or choose different ones.

Right-click the turtle to open the GUI, and run the label program by entering **label** in the command shell, followed by the words to set the turtle's name, which in this case are **set Sofonisba**. Then press ENTER:

```
> label set Sofonisba
Computer label set to "Sofonisba"
```

The words set Sofonisba are called *command line arguments*, and they tell the label program what do to. Together, the label program and set Sofonisba command line arguments form a *command* for the turtle to carry out.

The > symbol at the start of the code is called the *prompt*. We type our commands at the prompt, and after the turtle has carried them out, a new > prompt will appear and wait for our next command.

WARNING *You can mine the turtle with a pickaxe to put it in your inventory, but only do this after you've set a label for it. Otherwise, it will lose all its fuel and erase any programs it had. (Fuel is described in the next section.) Mining a turtle also causes it to drop its inventory, much like mining a chest.*

Now that the label program has set the turtle's name to Sofonisba, run the dance command to start another preloaded program:

```
> dance
Preparing to get down...
Press any key to stop the groove
```

Press ESC to close the turtle GUI. You'll see that as the dance program runs, the turtle bot randomly spins around. Right-click the turtle to bring up the turtle GUI again. The dance program is still running, but it is programmed to stop when you press any key. You can also stop any program by holding down CTRL-T for one full second while the GUI is open.

FUELING THE TURTLE

Turtles can move forward, backward, up, or down (and they can fly!). But
in order to move, they need fuel. Any items you can burn in a furnace can
be consumed as fuel, and one unit of fuel can move the turtle one block.
Table 2-1 shows how many units of fuel each item provides.

Table 2-1: Turtle Fuel Sources

Item	Item name	Units of fuel
	Stick	5
	Wooden tools (pickaxe, shovel, and so on)	10
	Wood	15
	Planks	15

Item	Item name	Units of fuel
	Coal or charcoal	80
	Blaze rod	120
	Coal block	800
	Lava bucket	1,000

The item that provides the most fuel is a bucket of lava. Notice that wood and planks both provide 15 fuel units. You can craft a wood block into four planks, so you can get four times as much fuel if you turn wood blocks into planks before you use them as fuel. In general, using coal or charcoal is usually the easiest way to fuel your turtles. Coal provides 80 fuel units, but coal blocks provide 800 units. Because it takes only nine coal items to craft a coal block, it's more efficient to craft coal into coal blocks before fueling. Blaze rods are rare (they're only dropped by defeated blaze mobs in the Nether) and don't give that much fuel, so you should save them for crafting instead.

A basic turtle can store up to 20,000 units of fuel. Only *moving* uses fuel. You don't need fuel for turning, mining, crafting, digging, and everything else a turtle does. Hovering in the air doesn't require fuel either; it's just like being on the ground.

To burn an item for fuel, it must be in the turtle's inventory and in the *selected slot*, which has a thick border around it, as shown in Figure 2-8.

When you have an item to burn in the selected slot, run the refuel program. If you have more than one item to burn for fuel, enter the number of items you want to burn after refuel.

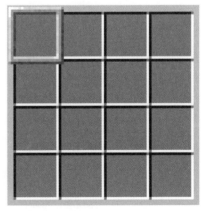

Figure 2-8: The currently selected slot of the turtle's inventory has a thicker border than the other slots.

For example, enter the following in the command shell:

```
> refuel 64
Fuel level is 5120
```

This command will run the refuel program and burn up to 64 items in the currently selected slot. The amount of fuel units this produces depends on the type of item in the slot. To find out how much fuel the turtle has, just run refuel 0:

```
> refuel 0
Fuel level is 5120
```

This command will display how much fuel the turtle has without burning any fuel items in the inventory.

WARNING *If you mine a turtle with a pickaxe to put it in your inventory before setting a label for the turtle, it will lose all the fuel it had. Be sure to run the label program to give it a label first.*

MOVING THE TURTLE

Now that the turtle is fueled up, let's move it. From the command shell, we can run the go program to tell it to move forward and backward. Enter the following into the command shell:

```
> go forward
```

When you press ESC to close the GUI, the turtle will have moved forward one space. Note that if a block is in front of the turtle blocking its path, the turtle will wait until it is cleared. If you want to terminate the program, hold down CTRL-T for a full second.

To tell the turtle to go backward, enter the following:

```
> go back
```

The turtle will move back one space. Enter a number after forward or back to move the turtle that number of spaces, as in the following example:

```
> go forward 2
```

The turtle will move forward two spaces.

Turning the turtle is similar. Enter the words left or right followed by a number to make the turtle turn left or right that number of times. For example, go left will make the turtle turn to face left. Entering go right 2 will make the turtle turn right twice so it's facing the opposite direction.

We can even chain multiple movements together, as in the following example:

```
> go forward 2 up right forward down back 3 left
```

The turtle will move forward two spaces, move up one space, turn right, move forward one space, move down one space, move back three spaces, and then turn left.

There are a few shortcut words you can use for the go program: fd for forward, bk for back, lt for left, rt for right, and dn for down. Enter the following example into the command shell:

```
> go fd 2 up rt fd dn bk 3 lt
```

This moves the turtle the same way the previous example did, except there is much less to type.

GETTING STARTED WITH LUA PROGRAMMING

Running the programs that turtles come with is useful, but the real power comes when you write your own programs in the Lua programming language. A *programming language* is a language that you can use to write instructions that a computer can understand. At this point, it might be difficult to determine what these instructions and programming words are used for, but keep in mind that they're just the building blocks for useful programs you'll make later. You'll learn these Lua instructions one at a time.

RUNNING THE LUA SHELL

Lua has a *Lua shell*, which allows you to enter and run Lua instructions in the turtle's GUI. You'll need to run the lua program to access it:

```
> lua
Interactive Lua prompt.
Call exit() to exit.
lua>
```

This command opens the Lua shell, as shown in Figure 2-9, and this is where you'll enter your Lua instructions. The Lua shell is handy for seeing what each instruction does because you can enter one instruction at a time, which saves a lot of work.

NOTE *In this book, the Lua shell is where you enter Lua code. It displays the lua> prompt at the front of each line where you enter your instructions in the Lua language. The command shell is where you enter commands to run programs. It has the simpler > prompt. It's easy to confuse the two. If you get error messages when you run your code, double-check which prompt you're using.*

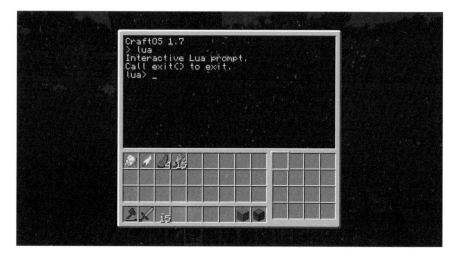

Figure 2-9: The Lua shell in the turtle's GUI

Let's start with a simple instruction that tells a turtle to turn left. Enter this instruction into the Lua shell:

```
lua> turtle.turnLeft()
true
```

As you type, Lua will autofill the instruction it thinks you're typing. You can press TAB to use the autocomplete suggestion and save time. In Figure 2-10, I've typed turtle.tu, and the autocomplete suggests turtle .turnLeft(. Pressing TAB will fill in the rnLeft(highlighted part, and then I can type the remaining).

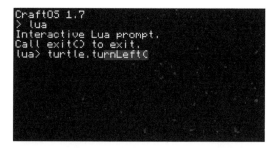

Figure 2-10: Autocomplete suggests turtle.turnLeft(when you enter turtle.tu.

The word true that appears after you enter the command is called a *return value*, and it lets you know the turtle was successfully able to turn left. Many turtle instructions will return true if they can carry out your instruction and false if they can't. (The true and false values are called *Boolean values* and are explained in Chapter 5.)

After returning true, the lua> prompt appears again, waiting for your next instruction. Press ESC to see that the turtle has turned to the left, as shown in Figure 2-11.

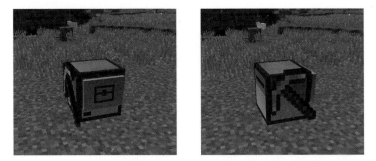

Figure 2-11: The turtle before and after running turtle.turnLeft()

Right-click the turtle to bring up the turtle's GUI again, and enter the following into the Lua shell:

```
lua> turtle.turnRight()
true
```

Now when you press ESC, you'll see that the turtle has turned to the right and is facing its original direction. The turtle.turnLeft() and turtle.turnRight() instructions are *functions*. In programming, a function is a kind of miniprogram inside a program. Functions contain a set of instructions to perform a small action. When a function is run as a Lua instruction, we say that we are *calling* the function.

The turtle.turnLeft() and turtle.turnRight() functions are in the turtle module. A *module* is a collection of functions. To call the functions inside the turtle module, you need to type turtle with a period before the function name. The turtle module has many functions for making the turtle move, mine, dig, place blocks, and do everything else. You'll learn many of these functions and modules throughout this book!

GOODBYE LUA: EXITING LUA'S PROMPT

Notice that pressing ESC will exit the GUI, but the next time you right-click the turtle, you'll still be in the Lua shell. You can exit the Lua shell and go back to the command shell prompt by calling the exit() function. Enter the following into the Lua shell:

```
lua> exit()
>
```

After exiting back to the command shell prompt, you'll see that the lua> prompt has been replaced with the command shell's > prompt.

LETTING LUA DO THE MATH

Don't worry if you think you're not good at math—Lua will do all the math for you! Lua can solve math problems just like a calculator if you give it the right instructions.

Return to the Lua prompt and enter the following:

```
lua> 2 + 2
4
```

We call these math problems *expressions*. The 2s in the expression are called *values*. Specifically, they are number values. The + sign in the expression is called an *operator*. When you give these values and operators to Lua as an expression, Lua will *evaluate* the expression to a single value, which is the answer to the math problem. The expression 2 + 2 evaluates to 4.

Spacing doesn't matter in an expression. You can use as many or as few spaces as you want. Enter the following into the Lua shell:

```
lua> 3+4
7
lua> 3        +    4
7
```

Even though you can use as many spaces as you like, most programmers will use a single space between values and operators to make their code easier to read.

Lua recognizes the math operators for addition (+), subtraction (-), multiplication (*), division (/), and exponentiation (^). Enter the following into the Lua shell to see examples of these operators in use:

```
lua> 100 + 1
101
lua> 10 - 4
6
lua> 7 * 5
35
lua> 21 / 3
7
lua> 3^2
9
```

Although some of these operations don't use the same symbols you would use in math class, they work in the same way.

A value by itself is also an expression: it evaluates to itself. Enter the following into the command shell to see an example:

```
lua> 42
42
```

You can see that the value 42 by itself evaluates to 42. Expressions always evaluate to a single value, even for a small expression like 42.

Expressions can be as long as you like. Enter the following into the Lua shell:

```
lua> 1 + 2 + 3 + 4 + 5
15
```

This expression has five values and four operators, but Lua can evaluate it to the single value 15. Lua evaluates the expression one step at a time, working from left to right, but you don't see all these steps on your computer.

ERROR! ERROR!

Notice that for multiplication, Lua uses the asterisk *, not the cross symbol or letter x. If you try to use x for multiplication, Lua will show an error:

```
lua> 5 x 5
bios.lua:14: [string "lua"]:1:
unexpected symbol
```

An error just means that Lua couldn't understand the instruction you gave it. Make sure your instruction is properly typed and enter it again.

Programming error messages can be confusing. If you don't understand what the message means, you can enter the error message (such as "unexpected symbol" in the example) into a search engine to find explanations for it.

ORDER OF OPERATIONS

The rules that determine which parts of an expression are evaluated first are called the *order of operations*. The order of operations in Lua is the same as the order of operations in mathematics. Going from left to right, operations in parentheses are done first, then the ^ operations, then the * and / operations, followed by the + and - operations. Enter the following into the command shell:

```
lua> 2 + 3 * 4
14
```

The expression 2 + 3 * 4 evaluates to 14 instead of 20 because the 3 * 4 evaluates to 12 first, making the expression 2 + 12, which evaluates to 14.

Lua evaluates this expression one step at a time, as shown here:

You can change the order of operations by using parentheses. Enter the following into the Lua shell:

```
lua> (2 + 3) * 4
20
```

Now the (2 + 3) part evaluates to 5 first, making the expression 5 * 4, which evaluates to 20. Lua evaluates this expression as shown here:

THAT'S SO RANDOM: GENERATING RANDOM NUMBERS

One other way Lua can help you do your math is by providing random numbers. Lots of games and programs use random numbers (think of how many board games use random numbers generated from rolling dice), so at times you'll need to generate random numbers for your programs, too. To do so, you'll use the math.random() function, which returns a random number every time you call it. Notice that the random() function is inside the math module. Enter the following into the Lua shell:

```
lua> math.random(1, 6)
6
lua> math.random(1, 6)
1
lua> math.random(1, 6)
1
lua> math.random(1, 6)
3
lua> math.random(100, 200)
142
```

Because the return values are random, your numbers will probably be different from the ones in this example. Notice that when we call the random() function, we include two numbers inside the parentheses. These values are the function call's *arguments*. Arguments are values given to the function call that tell the function how to behave. When you put arguments inside a function call's parentheses, you're *passing arguments* to the function call. The random() function takes two arguments: the minimum and maximum random number that the function call should return. When you pass 1 and 6 to the function call, the return value will always be between 1 and 6. When you pass it 100 and 200, the return value will be between 100 and 200.

Whenever you need to add a random element to your program, you'll use the random() function. We'll do this in the mydance program we'll write in Chapter 4.

STORING VALUES WITH VARIABLES

To use values multiple times, you can store them in variables. A *variable* is like a box in the computer's memory in which you can store a single value (see Figure 2-12). To make a variable, you write the variable name, followed by an equal sign (=), followed by the value you want to store in the variable. For example, if you wanted to keep track of how much coal you have, you could use the instruction coal = 10 to store the value 10 in a variable named coal. (Perhaps this variable keeps track of how much coal the turtle has mined.) This kind of instruction is called an *assignment statement*, and the equal sign (=) is called the *assignment operator*.

Figure 2-12: The instruction coal = 10 is like telling the program, "The variable coal now has the number value 10 in it."

You can use a variable in expressions wherever you would use the value of the variable. For example, enter the following into the Lua shell:

```
lua> coal = 10
lua> coal + 4
14
lua> coal + 10
20
lua> 12 - coal + 3
5
```

You set the coal variable to 10 on the first line. After you do this, the value 10 is used wherever you use coal.

You can put an expression on the right side of the assignment operator to assign the variable's value, too. The value that the expression evaluates to is then stored in the variable. When coal = 2 * 3 + 4, Lua calculates coal to be the value 10, as shown here:

Also, just like how a value by itself evaluates to itself, you can see what value is in a variable by entering the variable name into the Lua shell:

```
lua> coal
10
```

We previously assigned coal the number 10, so when we enter coal, it evaluates to the value 10.

Let's change the value stored in the coal variable using another assignment statement. This is called *overwriting* the variable. Enter the following into the Lua shell:

```
lua> coal = 100
lua> 2 + coal + 3
105
lua> coal = 200
lua> 2 + coal + 3
205
```

Variables can store only one value at a time. When a variable's value is overwritten with a new value, the old value is discarded and forgotten, as shown in Figure 2-13.

Figure 2-13: The coal variable is overwritten with the value 200, and the old 100 value is forgotten.

Once a variable has a value, you can use the variable in its own assignment statement. Using a different variable named counter, enter the following into the Lua shell:

```
❶ lua> counter = 0
   lua> counter
   0
❷ lua> counter = counter + 1
   lua> counter
❸ 1
❹ lua> counter = counter + 1
   lua> counter
   2
❺ lua> counter = counter + 100
   lua> counter
   102
```

You first assign counter the value of 0 ❶, and then assign counter to be equal to itself plus 1 ❷. The result is that counter is now equal to 1 ❸. You can continue adding 1 to counter ❹ by pressing the up arrow to display previous instructions, just like you did in the command shell. Adding 1 to counter lets you use counter to count up. This technique will be useful in your future programs when, for example, you need to count the number of times you've run a command. You can reassign counter as many times as you want, and you can even modify it with values other than 1, such as 100 ❺.

Variables are useful for storing the results of calculations or other data that you want to use later in a program. Most programs you'll write (and almost every program in this book) use variables.

VARIABLE NAMES

Variable names can be anything as long as they begin with a letter or underscore and consist of only letters, numbers, and underscores. Variable names usually describe the value they store, such as fuelPercentage, spaceLeft, or coal. Variable names are *case sensitive*, which means the same variable name in a different case is considered a different variable. The variables coal, Coal, and COAL are considered to be three different variables.

CHECKING THE TURTLE'S FUEL LEVELS

Let's use variables and expressions in the Lua shell to calculate the amount of coal needed to completely fuel the turtle. The turtle.getFuelLevel() function returns the current fuel level, and the turtle.getFuelLimit() function returns the maximum amount of fuel the turtle can hold. Enter the following into the Lua shell:

```
lua> turtle.getFuelLimit()
20000
```

```
      lua> turtle.getFuelLevel()
      968
❶ lua> spaceLeft = turtle.getFuelLimit() - turtle.getFuelLevel()
      lua> spaceLeft
      19032
❷ lua> coalNeeded = spaceLeft / 80
      lua> coalNeeded
      237.9
```

The expression turtle.getFuelLimit() - turtle.getFuelLevel() calculates the amount of space left in the turtle's fuel tank ❶. The value this expression evaluates to is stored in the spaceLeft variable. Because one coal item can fuel 80 units, the amount of coal needed is spaceLeft / 80. This value is stored in the coalNeeded variable ❷.

You can see how function calls, expressions, and variables can be combined into useful code for a turtle robot. As you learn more programming concepts, the code you create will become more sophisticated.

WHAT YOU LEARNED

In this chapter, you learned how to create and control turtles. Turtle robots can be crafted just like any other item in Minecraft, and they can be equipped with brand-new diamond tools. Turtles need to be fueled with items such as wood or coal to be able to move. Right-clicking the turtle brings up its GUI, which shows its inventory and command shell. The command shell is where you enter commands and programs. Turtles come with some programs, such as label, dance, and refuel.

You also learned some basic Lua programming with the Lua shell. The simplest type of Lua instructions are expressions, such as 2 + 2. Expressions are made up of values (like 2) and operators (like +), and they evaluate to a single value.

Lua code also includes functions, which are miniprograms inside your Lua program. By calling these functions, you can perform simple actions, such as turning the turtle around or generating a random number. Function calls evaluate to values, and these values are known as return values.

Values can be stored in variables to be used later in a program, and almost every program uses variables. You use an assignment statement, such as coal = 10, to store a value in a variable.

Although the programming concepts you've learned in this chapter may seem boring compared to making awesome robots, they're the building blocks of software. In Chapter 3, you'll use them in real programs.

3

TALKING TO YOUR TURTLE

IT'S ALIVE! In Chapter 2, you created your first turtle robot, fueled it, and brought it to life. Your robotic creation has a body, but it doesn't have much in the way of a brain. A Minecraft turtle's brain is its program, which tells it what to do. Without a program to run, your robot doesn't do anything. Let's give the robot a bit of personality by writing a program that lets us talk with it.

TEACHING YOUR TURTLE TO SAY HELLO!

We'll use the turtle's edit program to create a new file and write and edit our first program. Programs like the edit program, which we use to write other programs, are called *text editors*. Right-click the turtle to open its GUI, and then enter the following into the command shell:

```
> edit hello
```

Whenever you want to create or open a file, you'll write the keyword edit followed by the filename. The edit hello code runs the edit program and creates and opens a hello file to edit. In the file, we'll write the instructions for our program. The instructions will *all* run one after another instead of one at a time like when we were entering them into the Lua shell in Chapter 2. The hello program will display Hello, world! on the screen— a traditional program for new programmers to write.

Even though the text editor doesn't have a lot of room, you'll still be able to type long instructions on one line. To move the blinking cursor to other lines, use the keyboard keys listed in Table 3-1.

Table 3-1: Keyboard Keys to Move the Text Editor's Cursor

Keyboard keys	Cursor action
Up, Down, Left, Right	Moves the cursor in the key's direction
PgUp, PgDn	Moves the cursor several lines up or down at a time
Backspace	Erases the text behind the cursor
Delete	Erases the text in front of the cursor
Home	Moves the cursor to the start of the line
End	Moves the cursor to the end of the line
Tab	Can autocomplete an instruction you've started to type

A program's instructions are called its *source code*. Enter the following source code for the hello program into the editor, but don't type the number, period, and space at the beginning of each line. The line numbers are just used for reference in this book. I'll explain the code step by step in this chapter, so don't worry about what each line means for now.

hello
```
1. print('Hello, world!')
2. print('I am ' .. os.getComputerLabel())
3. print('What is your name?')
4. name = io.read()
5. textutils.slowPrint('Nice to meet you, ' .. name)
```

When you finish entering the code, press the CTRL key to bring up the Save/Exit menu at the bottom of the shell. The edit program will look like Figure 3-1 when the menu is open.

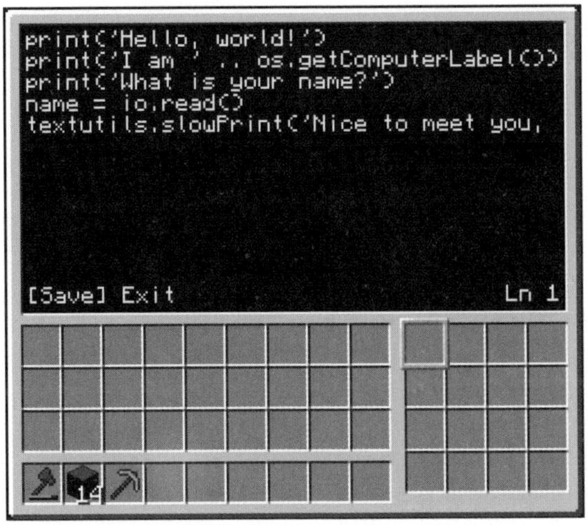

```
print('Hello, world!')
print('I am ' .. os.getComputerLabel())
print('What is your name?')
name = io.read()
textutils.slowPrint('Nice to meet you,
```

[Save] Exit   Ln 1

Figure 3-1: The hello program typed into the editor

The [Save] option has brackets around it to highlight it. Press ENTER to save the hello file on the turtle so you can access, edit, and run the program later. Then press CTRL to bring up the Save/Exit menu again. Press the right arrow key to highlight **[Exit]**, and press ENTER to take you out of the file and back to the command shell prompt.

RUNNING THE HELLO PROGRAM

In the command shell, you can run the hello program the same way you ran the label, dance, and refuel programs. Just enter hello in the command shell:

```
> hello
Hello, world!
I am Sofonisba
What is your name?
```

MY PROGRAM DIDN'T WORK!

If you see the error hello:1: attempt to concatenate string and nil when you run the program, you haven't named your turtle using the label program. From the shell's > prompt, run the label set Sofonisba command to set your turtle's name to Sofonisba. (You can also choose a different name.)

The turtle says hello, introduces itself, and waits for you to type your name. After I enter my name, Al, the program looks like this:

```
> hello
Hello, world!
I am Sofonisba
```

```
What is your name?
Al
Nice to meet you, Al
```

When the program finishes, it returns to the > prompt and is ready for you to run another program.

The software that runs programs written in the Lua programming language is called the *Lua interpreter*. We shorten the name of the interpreter and call it Lua, so *Lua* refers to both the programming language and the software that runs code written in that language. The place in the code where the Lua interpreter is currently running instructions is called the *execution*. The execution always starts at the first line of a program. It *executes* (or runs) the instruction on line 1. Then it moves down and executes each instruction, or line of source code.

Look at the text the program produced, and then look back at the hello program's source code. Before moving on to the explanation, try to figure out on your own what each line of code does. Try modifying the print('Hello, world!') line to print('Greetings') instead. Then save the program, exit the editor, and run the hello program again to see what changed. These are the steps you use to become a skilled programmer: guess what the code does, determine whether your guess is correct, figure out why your guess is incorrect (if it is), and experiment with the code to see what changes.

LISTING ALL FILES WITH THE LS COMMAND

If you forget which files you have on a turtle, you can run the ls (or "list," note the lowercase "l") command to list them. Enter the following into the command shell:

```
> ls
rom
hello
```

The ls command lists files, including programs, and folders that contain other files. The *rom* folder contains other files that come with the turtle, but we won't be using them in this book.

DISPLAYING TEXT WITH THE PRINT() FUNCTION

Let's look at the hello program line by line. The first line is as follows:

hello
```
1. print('Hello, world!')
```

This line is a function call to the print() function, which makes the Hello, world! text appear. You can experiment with the print() function at the Lua shell. Run the lua program, and enter the following.

```
lua> print('Hello, world!')
Hello, world!
1
```

When you want to determine how a piece of code works, you can enter it into the Lua shell to examine what it does. As you can see, the print() function displays text on the screen. The 1 at the end is the return value of the print() function, which is the number of lines of text that were printed. The 1 won't appear when you call the print() function in a program like hello. It only appears here because the Lua shell helpfully displays the return values of all functions.

Recall from Chapter 2 that the math.random() function took two values inside the parentheses when it was called. These arguments told the function the range for the random number it should return. The print() function also takes an argument, which in this case is 'Hello, world!'. This kind of text value is known as a string, which you'll learn about next.

THE STRING DATA TYPE

You've used number values, such as 2 and 10, in your programs, but you'll also want to use letters. *Strings* are a type of value that contain text instead of numbers. Similar to number values, strings can be stored in variables or used in expressions. Strings and numbers are the *data types* of these values. You'll learn about other data types, such as Booleans and nil, in Chapter 5.

Because strings are made up of letters that could look like Lua commands, Lua needs to know when a string value begins and ends so it doesn't confuse it as Lua code. Strings begin and end with a single quote ('), as in 'Hello, world!'. The single quote is not a part of the text; it just marks where the text begins and ends in your source code. You can also use double quotes ("), as in "Hello, world!".

You can also use a string value with no text at all between the two quotes: ''. This is called an *empty string*.

STRINGING STRINGS TOGETHER WITH CONCATENATION

Let's look at line 2 in the hello program's source code:

hello
```
2. print('I am ' .. os.getComputerLabel())
```

Line 2 has a call to the print() function, but the value we pass to print() has some new Lua code. The .. is called the *string concatenation operator*. It behaves like the + operator for numbers except it's for strings. Just like the + operator can combine two numbers together into a new number, the .. operator can *concatenate*, or combine, two string values into a single string. Enter the following into the Lua shell:

```
lua> 'Hello,' .. 'world!'
Hello,world!
```

This line of code is an expression, just like 2 + 2. 'Hello,' and 'world!' are values, and .. is an operator. Like all expressions, 'Hello,' .. 'world!' evaluates to a single value, which in this case is the string 'Hello,world!'.

Lua doesn't add spaces when you concatenate strings. Because neither of the two strings in our example had a space, there is no space between the words in the evaluated string. If you want a space between your text, you must add it to one of the two strings' values. For example, 'Hello, ' .. 'world!' or 'Hello,' .. ' world!' will evaluate to 'Hello, world!'.

Line 2 of the program concatenates the two strings 'I am ' and the string returned by a new function named os.getComputerLabel(). We'll look at how this function works in the next section.

RETRIEVING TURTLE NAMES

In Chapter 2, you set the turtle's name using the label program. Your programs can retrieve this name as a string value using the os.getComputerLabel() function. Function calls can be part of an expression, just like values, because a function call evaluates to its return value. Enter the following into the Lua shell to see how this function works:

```
lua> os.getComputerLabel()
Sofonisba
lua> turtleName = os.getComputerLabel()
lua> print(turtleName)
Sofonisba
1
```

The function call evaluates to a string value of the turtle's name, so turtleName = os.getComputerLabel() is the same as turtleName = 'Sofonisba'.

Take another look at line 2 in the hello program:

hello
```
2. print('I am ' .. os.getComputerLabel())
```

The expression 'I am ' .. os.getComputerLabel() concatenates the turtle's name with the string 'I am ' to evaluate to a single string. This single string is passed to the print() function, which is why I am Sofonisba appears on the screen when the program is run. Line 2 is just an expression that evaluates to a single value, as shown here:

```
print('I am ' .. os.getComputerLabel())

print('I am ' .. 'Sofonisba')

print('I am Sofonisba')

1
```

Remember that the print() function returns a value of the number of lines it printed, which is why it evaluates to 1. The string value that the print() function prints isn't its return value.

GETTING KEYBOARD INPUT WITH THE IO.READ() FUNCTION

Look at lines 3 and 4 in the hello program:

hello
```
3. print('What is your name?')
4. name = io.read()
```

Line 3 is another call to print(). But line 4 has a new function: io.read(). When called, the io.read() function pauses the program until the player types something and presses ENTER. The text the player inputs is returned from io.read() as a string, which is assigned to the variable name.

If the player entered Al, name would be assigned the string value 'Al'.

BONUS ACTIVITY: PROPER INTRODUCTIONS

You've written a *hello* program to tell the turtle your name, but you can also tell the turtle a bit more about yourself. Write a program where the turtle asks the player for not only their name but also their age and favorite video game. Save each of these responses in separate variables, and then use the print() function and .. operator to display them back to the player.

GIVING TEXT A TYPEWRITER EFFECT

You may have noticed when you ran the hello program that the text in the last line was displayed letter by letter as though it was slowly being typed with a typewriter. This is done using the textutils.slowPrint() function:

hello
```
5. textutils.slowPrint('Nice to meet you, ' .. name)
```

The argument to slowPrint() is the string 'Nice to meet you, ' concatenated with the string in the variable name, which is how the program says hello to the player using their name. Line 5 is the last line of code, so the program *terminates*, or quits, after it's executed.

CHANGING TURTLE NAMES

You can change the turtle's name by calling the os.setComputerLabel() function and passing it a string value. Enter the following code into the Lua shell.

```
lua> os.setComputerLabel('Elisabetta')
lua> os.getComputerLabel()
Elisabetta
```

Your turtle's name is now Elisabetta. You can rename your turtle as many times as you'd like using the os.setComputerLabel() function.

> ### BONUS ACTIVITY: A TURTLE BY ANY OTHER NAME
>
> Try writing your own version of the label program. You can run edit mylabel to create the file. Have your program call print() and io.read() to ask the player for the turtle's new name, and then pass that name to the os.setComputerLabel() function.

WHAT YOU LEARNED

In this chapter, we created a "Hello, world!" program, which is a customary first program for new programmers to make. This program can output text (using the print() and textutils.slowPrint() functions) and input text (using the io.read() function). In Lua, text takes the form of string values, which can be stored in variables or used in expressions, just like number values.

String values also have operators, just like number values. The .. string concatenation operator can combine multiple strings to form one new string.

The hello program in this chapter was just the first step in writing programs for your robots. In Chapter 4, you'll learn a few more concepts and functions to make the turtle move (and dance!) around.

4

PROGRAMMING TURTLES
TO DANCE

Now that our turtles can talk, let's make them walk. Or even better, let's make them dance! Although turtles come with a program called dance, it's a simple program that only makes the turtles turn randomly. In this chapter, you'll create a much better turtle dancing program. The steps will look like Figure 4-1.

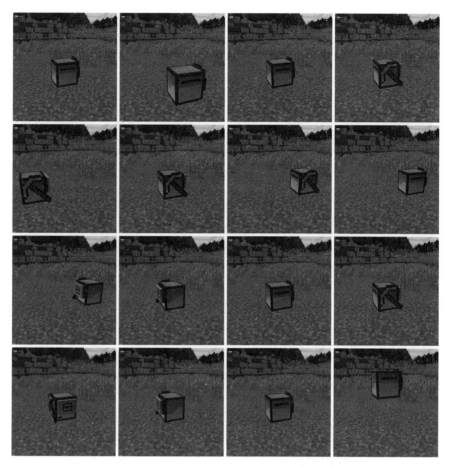

Figure 4-1: The turtle's dance steps

WRITING A DANCE PROGRAM

Using the text editor, create a program named mydance by entering **edit mydance** in the command shell. In the text editor, enter the following lines of code. Remember not to type the line numbers because they're just for reference.

mydance

```
1. --[[Dance program by Al Sweigart
2. Make the turtle dance!]]
3.
4. print('Time to dance!')
5.
6. -- Turtle starts dancing
7. turtle.forward()
8. turtle.back()
```

```
 9. turtle.turnRight()
10. turtle.forward()
11. turtle.back()
12. turtle.back()
13. turtle.turnLeft()
14. turtle.turnLeft()
15. turtle.back()
16. turtle.turnRight()
17.
18. -- Turtle spins around
19. for i = 1, 4 do
20.    turtle.turnRight()
21. end
22.
23. turtle.up()
24. turtle.down()
25. print('Done.')
```

After you've entered all these instructions, save the program by pressing the CTRL button, making sure **[Save]** is selected, and pressing ENTER. Then quit the editor by pressing CTRL, selecting **[Exit]**, and pressing ENTER.

RUNNING THE MYDANCE PROGRAM

After exiting the editor, run the mydance program in the command shell:

```
> mydance
Time to dance!
Done.
```

The text Time to dance! will appear onscreen. When the robot is done dancing, the text Done. will appear. Press ESC immediately after you run the program and before the text Done. appears to watch the turtle do a little dance. Every step the turtle takes is one that you programmed! Figure 4-2 shows how the turtle moves in response to the turtle.forward() and turtle.back() function calls on lines 7 and 8.

Figure 4-2: The turtle's first two dance moves

Let's look at each instruction in the mydance program.

USING COMMENTS IN YOUR CODE

The first two lines in the program contain a *comment*. Lua ignores comments because they're just notes for the programmer. This comment describes what the program does and who wrote the program.

mydance

```
1. --[[Dance program by Al Sweigart
2. Make the turtle dance!]]
3.
4. print('Time to dance!')
5.
6. -- Turtle starts dancing
```

The comment in this program that begins on line 1 and continues on line 2 is a *multiline comment* because it extends beyond one line. Multiline comments begin with --[[and continue until a]] appears.

Line 4 calls the print() function and makes Time to dance! appear in the command shell when you run the program. You learned about the print() function in Chapter 3.

Line 6 is also a comment, but it's a *single-line comment*. The comment starts at -- and ends at the end of the line instead of spanning multiple lines. Lua ignores the Turtle starts dancing text, which describes what the code that follows line 6 does, because it's a note for whoever is reading the program.

TURTLE MOVEMENT FUNCTIONS

After line 6, the next several lines of code in mydance call functions that make the turtle move.

mydance

```
6. -- Turtle starts dancing
7. turtle.forward()
8. turtle.back()
9. turtle.turnRight()
10. turtle.forward()
11. turtle.back()
12. turtle.back()
13. turtle.turnLeft()
14. turtle.turnLeft()
15. turtle.back()
16. turtle.turnRight()
```

You learned about the turtle.turnLeft() and turtle.turnRight() functions in Chapter 2. There are four other functions for moving the turtle that you haven't seen yet: turtle.up(), turtle.down(), turtle.forward(), and turtle.back().

EXPERIMENTING WITH MOVING THE TURTLE

Let's experiment with these movement functions in the Lua shell! Make sure you're in the correct shell (the prompt will be lua> instead of >), and run the following instructions:

```
lua> turtle.up()
true
lua> turtle.down()
true
lua> turtle.forward()
true
lua> turtle.back()
true
```

Remember to include turtle. in front of the direction names, and be sure the turtle has fuel. The functions turtle.up() and turtle.down() move the turtle up into the air and back down toward the ground. The functions turtle.forward() and turtle.back() move the turtle forward in the direction it is currently facing and then backward in the opposite direction. You can see these movements in Figure 4-3.

Figure 4-3: Experimenting with the turtle's movement functions

If the turtle is able to move in the direction you instruct it to, the function call will have a return value of true. (The values true and false are values of the Boolean data type, which I'll explain in Chapter 5.)

With the turtle already on the ground, call the turtle.down() function in the Lua shell, like this:

```
lua> turtle.down()
false
Movement obstructed
```

Because a block is in the way, the turtle won't be able to move, and the turtle.down() function call will return false and a string value that displays an error message. If the turtle is out of fuel, the movement will also fail, but a different message will be displayed:

```
lua> turtle.forward()
false
Out of fuel
```

These functions tell you the reason the turtle couldn't move. You'll call these movement functions often in this book's programs to move the turtle.

LOOPING WITH FOR LOOPS

So far, the mydance program's execution, also known as the *flow of execution*, has started at the top of the source code and moved straight down, executing each line of code. However, we can make the execution loop over a group of instructions several times. Instructions that alter the normal line-by-line sequential flow of execution are called *flow control statements*.

Enter the following line of code into the Lua shell to see one type of flow control statement called the for loop:

```
lua> for i = 1, 4 do print(i) end
1
2
3
4
```

The instruction you entered is a for loop statement. A for loop can execute a group of instructions several times. This group, which is the code between the do and end keywords, is called a *block*, and each execution of the block is called an *iteration*. The block in the example is made up of the print(i) function call. (Programmers often use the variable name i in for loops. It stands for "iteration.") A block can be made up of several lines of code, but in this case the block is simple and has just one function call. This for loop tells Lua to execute this block four times because the 1, 4 tells the loop to iterate from 1 to 4.

The statement for i = 1, 4 do print(i) end prints the numbers 1 to 4. The first time Lua executes the code in the block, the i variable is set to 1, which evaluates to print(1), displaying 1 on the screen. This is the first iteration of the for loop. When the execution reaches the end of the code in the block, it moves back up to the start of the block to run the code a second time. On this second iteration, 1 is added to the i variable so it's set to 2, and 2 is printed to the screen. The execution continues to loop until i is set to 4 on the fourth and final iteration, which is the number after the comma in the for loop statement.

We can supply any two numbers to the for loop. For example, enter the following into the Lua shell to make a for loop iterate from 10 to 13:

```
lua> for i = 10, 13 do print(i) end
10
11
12
13
```

We can also specify a third number, which is called the *step number*. Instead of increasing by 1 after each iteration, we can make the for loop increase or decrease the loop's variable by any amount. Enter the following into the Lua shell:

```
lua> for i = 10, 20, 2 do print(i) end
10
12
14
16
18
20
```

This line of code makes the step number 2, so Lua will print all the even numbers between 10 and 20.

We can also use negative numbers in a for loop to make the loop count down from the starting number. In the following line of code, we use a step number of -1:

```
lua> for i = 4, 1, -1 do print(i) end
4
3
2
1
```

This code makes the for loop count down from 4 to 1. Try changing the step number to -2 to see what happens. Using for loops is a simple way to execute a group of instructions multiple times. You'll learn other flow control statements in Chapter 5.

TAKING THE TURTLE FOR A SPIN

Let's return to the mydance program. Lines 19 to 21 use a for loop to make the turtle spin:

mydance
```
18. -- Turtle spins around
19. for i = 1, 4 do
20.    turtle.turnRight()
21. end
```

When we use for loops in programs, it's common to *indent* (that is, add spaces to the beginning of) each line of code in the loop's block. Indenting code lines makes it easier to see which lines are inside which blocks, especially when you start adding blocks inside other blocks (we'll do this in Chapter 5). The end keyword is at the same level of indentation as the for keyword, making it easy to see where the loop begins and ends.

Line 20, which turns the turtle to the right, executes four times, making the turtle do a complete 360 degree spin. If you changed line 19 to for i = 1, 8 do, you could make the turtle perform two complete spins like in Figure 4-4.

Figure 4-4: A turtle does two spins by turning right eight times.

DOING A LITTLE HOP

Finally, in lines 23 and 24, the turtle will do a little hop by moving up and then back down:

mydance

```
23. turtle.up()
24. turtle.down()
25. print('Done.')
```

This hop looks like Figure 4-5. The last line of the program prints Done., and because there's no more code after line 25, the program terminates.

Figure 4-5: The turtle does a hop when turtle.up() and turtle.down() are called.

BONUS ACTIVITY: NEW DANCE MOVES

Try creating your own dance steps for the turtle. You can use the moving and turning functions to make the turtle hop, spin, and dance according to your own choreography!

SHARING AND DOWNLOADING PROGRAMS ONLINE

After you've entered your program into the turtle, you might want to share it with your friends. To copy programs from your turtle to the internet, you can use a *pastebin* website where people share text online by copying and pasting it to the website. You can upload your turtle programs as text to *https://pastebin.com/*, a popular pastebin site, by using the pastebin program that comes with all turtles. Enter the following into the command shell to upload mydance:

```
> pastebin put mydance
Connecting to pastebin.com... Success.
Uploaded as
https://pastebin.com/BLCJbpQJ
Run "pastebin get BLCJbpQJ" to download
anywhere
```

After uploading the program, the *https://pastebin.com/* website will generate a new, unique web address for it. When I ran the pastebin program, it told me the mydance program was successfully uploaded to *https://pastebin.com/BLCJbpQJ/*. Now anyone can see this program by opening a web browser to that site. You can also download this program to your turtle by entering the following into the command shell:

```
> pastebin get BLCJbpQJ mydance
Connecting to pastebin.com... Success.
Downloaded as mydance
```

The get BLCJbpQJ mydance command line argument tells pastebin that you want to get the program at *https://pastebin.com/BLCJbpQJ/* and save it on the turtle as mydance. Now you have a way to upload and download files to share them with others.

If the pastebin program displays the message Connecting to pastebin.com... Failed. when you run it, double-check that you typed the command line argument (BLCJbpQJ or whatever address was assigned to your pastebin) correctly and that you're connected to the internet. If the pastebin program displays File already exists, you need to first delete the existing mydance program, which is covered next.

DELETING FILES OFF THE TURTLE

When you ran the pastebin program, you told it to download the file, save it on the turtle, and name the file mydance. But if a program already exists with this name (such as the one you created with edit mydance), you'll either need to choose a different name or delete the existing mydance program.

To delete a program off the turtle, run the delete command followed by the name of the program to delete. For example, enter the following into the command shell:

```
> delete mydance
```

This line deletes the mydance program. Now you can run pastebin get BLCJbpQJ mydance to download the program from the internet.

PASTEBIN.COM LIMITATIONS

Keep in mind that for each Minecraft server, the *https://pastebin.com/* website allows *only* 25 new "pastes" per day. This limitation can make it difficult to update pastes with new changes to your programs if lots of players are on your server.

TURTLEAPPSTORE.COM

You can also share your programs online without limitations at *https://turtleappstore.com/*. Instead of using the pastebin program, you can use the appstore program. Download the appstore program by running pastebin get iXRkjNsG appstore in the command shell:

```
> pastebin get iXRkjNsG appstore
Connecting to pastebin.com... Success.
Downloaded as appstore
```

The appstore program will download programs to your turtle just like the pastebin program does. For example, you can run appstore get AlSweigart mydance to download the mydance program from the AlSweigart appstore on the *https://turtleappstore.com/* website.

To upload your programs to the appstore and browse programs others have made, go to the *https://turtleappstore.com/* website and sign up for a free account. You'll find programs written by others, and you can learn from their code! This website also contains all the programs in this book.

BONUS ACTIVITY: MAZE RUNNER

Build a small maze out of some blocks, like in Figure 4-6, and then write a program for the turtle to run through it. You'll have to plan out the exact path for the turtle to take through the maze. If the turtle gets stuck, you can always start over by mining the turtle and moving it back to the start of the maze.

Figure 4-6: A turtle at the start of a small maze

WHAT YOU LEARNED

In this chapter, you learned several new programming concepts. You learned how to use comments to make notes that Lua will ignore. These comments can serve as reminders or describe what different parts of your program do. Single-line comments begin with --, and multiline comments begin with --[[and end with]].

You learned how to move the turtle with the movement functions: `turtle.forward()`, `turtle.back()`, `turtle.turnLeft()`, `turtle.turnRight()`, `turtle.up()`, and `turtle.down()`.

This chapter covered a new type of flow control statement called the for loop. These loops let you execute the same block of code a certain number of times.

You can use the `pastebin` program that comes with ComputerCraft turtles to share programs online at *https://pastebin.com/*. The appstore program at *https://turtleappstore.com/* provides some additional features as well.

In Chapter 5, we'll expand on the `mydance` program and use some new flow control statements, data types, and operators. With this knowledge, you'll be ready to automate Minecraft chores with turtles!

5

MAKING A BETTER DANCER

The dancing program in Chapter 4 was fairly simple and always instructed your turtle to do the same dance moves. In this chapter, we'll create a new program that makes the turtle do a variety of random moves. While creating this program, you'll learn about while loops, the Boolean and nil data types, and how to run or skip code blocks based on conditions.

WRITING A BETTER DANCE PROGRAM

Run the text editor by entering **edit mydance2** into the command shell. In the text editor, enter the following lines of code, but don't type the line numbers because they're only used here for reference:

mydance2

```
1. --[[A Better Dance program by Al Sweigart
2. Make the turtle dance better!]]
```

```
 3.
 4. local isUp = false
 5. local isBack = false
 6. local danceMove
 7. print('Hold Ctrl-T to stop dancing.')
 8. while true do
 9.    danceMove = math.random(1, 5)
10.
11.    if danceMove == 1 then
12.       -- turn left
13.       print('Turn to the left!')
14.       turtle.turnLeft()
15.
16.    elseif danceMove == 2 then
17.       -- turn right
18.       print('Turn to the right!')
19.       turtle.turnRight()
20.
21.    elseif danceMove == 3 then
22.       -- forward/back moves
23.       if isBack then
24.          print('Move forward!')
25.          turtle.forward()
26.          isBack = false
27.       else
28.          print('Move back!')
29.          turtle.back()
30.          isBack = true
31.       end
32.
33.    elseif danceMove == 4 then
34.       -- up/down moves
35.       if isUp then
36.          print('Get down!')
37.          turtle.down()
38.          isUp = false
39.       else
40.          print('Get up!')
41.          turtle.up()
42.          isUp = true
43.       end
44.
45.    else
46.       -- spin around
47.       print('Spin!')
48.       for i = 1, 4 do
49.          turtle.turnLeft()
50.       end
51.    end
52. end
```

After you've entered all these instructions, press CTRL, make sure **[Save]** is selected, and press ENTER. Then quit the editor by pressing CTRL, selecting **[Exit]**, and then pressing ENTER.

RUNNING THE MYDANCE2 PROGRAM

After exiting the editor, run the mydance2 program in the command shell. Press ESC shortly after running the program and watch the turtle do random dance moves. This program will continue running until you terminate it by holding down CTRL-T for a full second. When you've stopped the program, return to the command prompt to see output similar to the following:

```
> mydance2
Hold Ctrl-T to stop dancing.
Spin!
Get down!
Move back!
Move forward!
Spin!
Get up!
Turn to the left!
Terminated
```

Figure 5-1 shows the turtle doing its spin move.

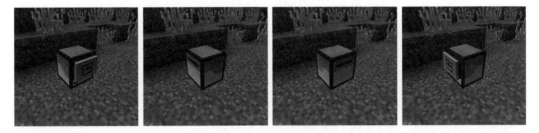

Figure 5-1: The spinning turtle

If you get errors when running this program, carefully compare your code to the code in this book to find any typos. If you still cannot fix your program, delete the file by running delete mydance2 and then download it by running pastebin get QAHOuYqS mydance2.

The mydance2 program uses Booleans, nil, while loops, if statements, and more. Let's look at it step by step.

THE BOOLEAN DATA TYPE

The program's first couple of lines contain comments that explain what the program is and who wrote it. Lines 4 and 5 are assignment statements:

mydance2
```
1. --[[A Better Dance program by Al Sweigart
2. Make the turtle dance better!]]
3.
4. local isUp = false
5. local isBack = false
```

The values assigned to the isUp and isBack variables are false and false. You can tell these aren't strings because they don't start and end with single quotes. Rather, these are *Boolean values*, which are another data type. Boolean values, or Booleans, are always either true or false. ("Boolean" is capitalized, unlike "string" or "number," because it's named after the 19th-century mathematician George Boole.)

Some of the turtle dance moves involve moving up and also moving backward. To prevent the turtle from moving too far away from its original position, we use the isUp and isBack variables to keep track of whether the turtle has already moved up or back. Although we set up these variables at the beginning of the program, we won't use them until later in the program.

THE NIL DATA TYPE

Notice that line 6 declares the danceMove variable without assigning it any value:

mydance2

```
6. local danceMove
```

Even though it isn't written in the code, danceMove is automatically assigned a value called nil. The nil value is the only value in the data type, which is also called nil. This value represents *no value* or the *lack of a value*. Any local statement that doesn't assign a value to the declared variable assigns nil. Line 6 is the same as writing local danceMove = nil.

LOOPING WITH WHILE LOOPS

In addition to the for loop, another kind of loop is the while loop. A *while loop* repeatedly executes a block of code as long as some condition is true. A *condition* is an expression that can be true or false. The condition is checked as part of a while statement, and the block of code that it executes is the action we want it to do when the condition is true.

Line 7 displays a reminder to the player that they can terminate the program by holding down CTRL-T, and line 8 is the while statement:

mydance2

```
7. print('Hold Ctrl-T to stop dancing.')
8. while true do
9.    danceMove = math.random(1, 5)
```

The while statement consists of the while keyword, followed by a condition (in this case, true) and the do keyword to mark the beginning of the block. The instructions are inside the block of code starting at line 9. The end of the block is marked with the end keyword. (Because the block is long, this code snippet shows only the first line of the block and doesn't show the end keyword, which is on line 31.) When the execution reaches the end keyword, it moves to the top of the block and checks the condition again. It continues looping through the code as long as the condition evaluates to `true`. If the condition is ever `false`, the execution moves past the `while` loop's block.

Figure 5-2 shows an example `while` loop.

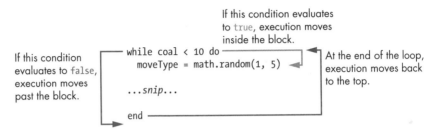

If this condition evaluates to `true`, execution moves inside the block.

If this condition evaluates to `false`, execution moves past the block.

At the end of the loop, execution moves back to the top.

```
while coal < 10 do
    moveType = math.random(1, 5)

...snip...

end
```

Figure 5-2: The execution of a `while` loop

The `while` loop continues to loop as long as the condition isn't `false` or `nil`. Many conditions use comparison operators, such as `coal < 10` in this example, which tests if the value in the `coal` variable is less than 10. (You'll learn more about comparison operators later in this chapter.) Conditions that use comparison operators can evaluate to `true` or `false`. If a condition evaluates to a number or string value (for example, some functions will return number values), it is considered the same as being `true`.

Remember that an expression can be made up of just a single value, in which case the expression evaluates to itself. Recall in Chapter 2 that when you entered the value 42 into the Lua shell, it evaluated to the value 42. The condition on line 8 of the `mydance2` program is just the `true` value. Because this expression always evaluates to `true`, the `while` loop will loop forever until the user stops it by terminating the program. This kind of never-ending loop is called an *infinite loop*. We use an infinite loop in this program because we want the turtle to keep dancing until we hold down CTRL-T to terminate the program.

The turtle has five different dance moves, and the program randomly chooses one based on the value in `danceMove`. Line 9 calls the `math.random()` function to create a random number between 1 and 5, and it stores this random number in the `danceMove` variable.

MAKING DECISIONS WITH IF STATEMENTS

Recall that the flow of execution is the order in which lines of code are executed. The normal flow of execution in our programs is from the top down. Loops such as `for` loops or `while` loops are considered flow control statements because they can make the execution move back up to the beginning of the loop.

An `if` statement is another kind of flow control statement. Line 11 uses an `if` statement, which executes a block of code only if its condition evaluates to `true`, as in the following.

```
11.    if danceMove == 1 then
12.       -- turn left
13.       print('Turn to the left!')
14.       turtle.turnLeft()
15.
16.    elseif danceMove == 2 then
```

An if statement is made up of the if keyword followed by a condition and the then keyword, which marks the beginning of the code block. Line 12 starts the instructions inside the code block that should execute if the condition is true. An elseif, else, or end keyword marks the end of the if statement's code block. In this case, on line 16 the block ends with the elseif keyword, which you'll learn more about shortly.

The condition on line 11 also contains code that will be unfamiliar to you because it uses a comparison operator. To better understand how if statements work, let's look at comparison operators next.

COMPARING TWO VALUES WITH COMPARISON OPERATORS

Comparison operators check a condition by comparing two values and evaluate to a Boolean true or false value. The condition on line 11 is danceMove == 1, which includes the "is equal to" (==) comparison operator. The == operator checks whether the values before it and after it are equal to each other, and returns true if they are or false if they're not. If the danceMove variable is equal to the value 1, the code on lines 12, 13, and 14 (between the then and elseif keywords) executes. This prints Turn to the left! on the GUI and makes the turtle turn left.

Be careful not to mix up the "is equal to" operator (==) and the assignment operator (=). The comparison operator == checks whether the values on either side of the operator are the same and returns true if they are, whereas the assignment operator = assigns the value on the right side of the operator to the variable on the left side of the operator.

Table 5-1 describes Lua's comparison operators.

Table 5-1: Comparison Operators in Lua

Comparison operator	Description
==	Is equal to
~=	Is not equal to
>	Is greater than
<	Is less than
>=	Is greater than or equal to
<=	Is less than or equal to

Let's experiment by entering the following operators into the Lua shell:

---

❶ ```
lua> 2 == 2
true
lua> 4 == 2 + 2
true
```
❷ ```
lua> 2 ~= 3
true
lua> 2 < 3
true
lua> 3 < 3
```
❸ ```
false
lua> 3 > 2
true
lua> 2 >= 2
true
```
❹ ```
lua> 2 + 9 * 2 == (25 - 15) * 2
true
```

As you can see, an expression with comparison operators always evaluates to a Boolean true or false value. The "is equal to" operator (==) compares two values and returns true if they are equal ❶. The "is not equal to" operator (~=) returns true if they aren't equal ❷. The "less than" (<) and "greater than" (>) operators work just like they do in math class. They compare whether the value next to the open part of the operator is bigger than the value on the other side of the operator and return true when that is the case. But if the values on both sides of the operator are equal to each other or if the value next to the open part of the operator is smaller than the value on the other side of the operator, the comparison will return false ❸.

The "greater than or equal to" (>=) and "less than or equal to" (<=) operators will do the same comparison as the less than and greater than operators but will return true if the values on both sides of the operator are equal to each other.

You can also use comparison operators to compare expressions, such as 2 + 9 * 2 == (25 - 15) * 2 ❹. When you see this type of expression, you can evaluate it one piece at a time, as shown here:

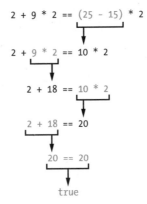

In the end, the expression will always evaluate to just true or false.

MAKING ALTERNATE DECISIONS WITH ELSEIF STATEMENTS

You can add an elseif statement to the end of an if block. In fact, an elseif statement works almost exactly like an if statement. They both include their own keyword (if or elseif), a condition, and the then keyword, which marks the beginning of the block. The execution instructions are inside the code block, and an elseif, else, or end keyword marks the end of the block.

The elseif statement must be paired with an if statement and only executes its code block when the if statement's condition is false but the elseif statement's condition is true. In plain English it means, "If this is true, do this, or else if this other thing is true, do that." If neither condition is true, neither block executes and the next part of the code executes.

Lines 17 to 19 execute if the condition in line 11, danceMove == 1, is false, and the condition in line 16, danceMove == 2, is true:

mydance2
```
16.    elseif danceMove == 2 then
17.       -- turn right
18.       print('Turn to the right!')
19.       turtle.turnRight()
20.
21.    elseif danceMove == 3 then
```

If the danceMove variable is set to 2 on line 9, the program prints Turn to the right! and turns the turtle to the right.

NESTED CODE BLOCKS

Another elseif statement is on line 21 for when danceMove is set to 3. Inside the elseif statement's block is another if statement on line 23 and its block, which starts at line 24 and ends at line 26. Putting a block inside another block of code is called *nesting*. Notice that because lines 24 to 26 are inside a new block, the code is indented by two more spaces. This indentation isn't required, but it does make the code easier to read.

mydance2
```
21.    elseif danceMove == 3 then
22.       -- forward/back moves
23.       if isBack then
24.         print('Move forward!')
25.         turtle.forward()
26.         isBack = false
```

The if statement nested in the elseif block executes only when the elseif statement's condition is true. We need a nested if statement because the dance move on line 21 is different from the others. This dance move makes the turtle move forward, but we don't want the turtle to keep moving forward; otherwise, it might wander away! So we check whether the turtle has already moved forward and, if it has, move the turtle backward instead. We do this using the nested if statement, which uses the isBack variable in its condition. We set up the isBack variable at the start of the program and use it to store a Boolean that indicates whether the turtle is back to where it originally started.

Remember that a variable can be used in an expression because it evaluates to the value inside it. So if isBack is set to true, then the condition on line 23 is true and lines 24 to 26 execute, which moves the turtle forward and sets isBack to false.

INDENTATION

Indentation in Lua source code is optional, but adding spaces to the beginning of lines makes them easier to read. You can immediately identify where code blocks begin and end by looking at the indentation. Compare the following code listings: the one on the left has indentations; the one on the right does not:

```
-- This code is easier to read!
if isBack then
    print('Move forward!')
    turtle.forward()
    isBack = false
else
    print('Move back!')
    turtle.back()
    isBack = true
end
```

```
-- This code is harder to read.
if isBack then
print('Move forward!')
turtle.forward()
isBack = false
else
print('Move back!')
turtle.back()
isBack = true
end
```

You can clearly see where the blocks of code are in the left code listing. But on the right, it's more difficult to find the else and end statements to know where the blocks end. Indenting your code is best practice.

MAKING A DECISION . . . OR ELSE!

Line 27 is an else statement, which ends the if statement's block. The block after an else statement executes if *all* of the previous if and elseif conditions are false. In plain English it means, "If this is true, do this, or else if it's false, do that." In this case, the else statement is paired with the if statement on line 23 but not with the if or elseif statements on lines 11, 16, and 21. The reason is that the else statement is also nested in the elseif statement on line 21, meaning that it executes only if the condition on line 21 is true.

Lines 28 to 30 execute if the condition on line 23 is false. The block after an else statement ends when the program reaches an end keyword. The else block runs only if all the previous if and elseif statements are false, so it has no condition.

mydance2

```
27.    else
28.        print('Move back!')
29.        turtle.back()
30.        isBack = true
31.    end
```

If isBack is set to false, lines 28 to 30 execute, which prints Move back! on the turtle's GUI, moves the turtle backward, and then sets isBack to true.

Notice that if isBack is true, the program sets it to false. If isBack is false, the program sets it to true. As a result, each time danceMove is set to 3 the turtle alternates between moving forward and backward. So the turtle never goes too far backward or too far forward and always moves between two positions.

MOVING UP AND DOWN

Line 33 is an elseif statement that checks whether danceMove is equal to 4. Notice that because the if statement on line 23 (if isBack then) is nested in the previous elseif block, the program will skip it if the execution moves to the elseif statement on line 33. This means that the elseif statement on line 33 is paired with the if statement on line 11.

mydance2

```
33.    elseif danceMove == 4 then
34.      -- up/down moves
35.      if isUp then
36.        print('Get down!')
37.        turtle.down()
38.        isUp = false
39.      else
40.        print('Get up!')
41.        turtle.up()
42.        isUp = true
43.      end
```

The code on lines 35 to 43 is similar to the code on lines 23 to 31. If danceMove is 4, the nested if statement on line 35 runs its block if isUp is true. Otherwise, the else statement on line 39 runs its block.

The program uses isBack and isUp to keep track of what kind of move to make when danceMove is 3 or 4. The if, elseif, and else statements direct where the execution of the program goes based on these three variables.

Figure 5-3 shows the turtle moving up and down.

Figure 5-3: The turtle moving up and down

SPINNING ALL AROUND

Another else statement is on line 45, and it's paired with the if statement on line 11. If every condition for the if and elseif statements on lines 11, 16, 21, 33, and 45 are false, the block after the else statement will run:

```
8. while true do
9.    danceMove = math.random(1, 5)
10.
11.    if danceMove == 1 then

       ...snip...

45.    else
46.       -- spin around
47.       print('Spin!')
48.       for i = 1, 4 do
49.          turtle.turnLeft()
50.       end
51.    end
52. end
```

In this block (which ranges from lines 46 to 51), the turtle prints Spin! to its GUI and enters a loop that makes the turtle turn left four times. This spin leaves the turtle facing its original direction.

Lines 50, 51, and 52 are all end statements. By looking at the indentation, we can match these end statements with the statements they're paired with, as follows:

- Line 50 is the end of the block started by the for statement on line 48.
- Line 51 is the end of the block started by the else statement on line 45.
- Line 52 is the end of the block started by the while statement on line 8.

Remember that one and only one of the blocks following the if, elseif, and else statements executes. The execution skips the rest. So after one of these blocks is run, the execution moves past the end statement on line 51. The next line is the end statement for the while loop, so the execution moves back to line 8 and rechecks the while statement's condition. Because this condition is just the value true, the execution will always reenter the block and do another random dance move.

Due to the infinite loop, there is no natural way for this program to end. The turtle will keep dancing forever until you hold down CTRL-T to terminate the program.

WHAT YOU LEARNED

In this chapter, you learned about while loops and conditions, which allow you to run the same code repeatedly. You also learned how to use conditions with if, elseif, and else statements and comparison operators to execute or skip code. These flow control statements allow you to program software to make decisions that direct how your turtle behaves. Comparison operators evaluate to one of the two Boolean values: true or false. The nil data type just has one value, nil, which represents a lack of value.

Of course, if you want smarter turtles, you'll have to use more than just a few if statements and loops in your code. But you have a good start with your dancing turtle!

PROGRAMMING A ROBOT LUMBERJACK

It's time to put your new programming knowledge to the test in the world of Minecraft. We'll program our first turtle to chop down all the wood blocks of a tree. With the help of these turtles, your wood supply problems will be over!

Chopping trees by hand in Minecraft has many problems. It's slow, it wears out your tools, and you need to reach the topmost wood block to completely chop down a tree. In comparison, turtles can harvest a wood block in one chop, their tools don't wear out, and they can hover as high as you need them to, as shown in Figure 6-1.

Figure 6-1: Four turtles chopping a tall jungle tree

Before we can write our tree-chopping program, you need to learn some additional turtle functions and you need to think about how the program will work.

EQUIPPING TURTLES WITH TOOLS

To chop down trees, you need to equip the turtle with a brand-new diamond tool. You can equip turtles with diamond pickaxes, shovels, axes, hoes, or swords, but an iron tool or a used diamond tool won't work. Fortunately, a tool's durability will never decrease once a turtle is equipped with it.

To equip a turtle with a tool, place the tool in the turtle's currently selected inventory slot, or *current slot*. This is the inventory slot with the thick border around it. Craft a diamond pickaxe and place it in the turtle's current slot. Run the Lua shell by entering the following:

```
> lua
Interactive Lua prompt.
Call exit() to exit.
```

Then, equip your turtle with the selected item by running this command:

```
lua> turtle.equipLeft()
```

Turtles can equip up to two tools: one on their left side and the other on their right. If you want to unequip a turtle, just call the turtle.equipLeft() or turtle.equipRight() function with nothing in the currently selected slot. The turtle will remove the tool and put it in its inventory.

Turtles can equip any diamond tool, but the diamond pickaxe is the most versatile. The diamond shovel can mine dirt blocks and the diamond axe can mine wood blocks, but neither can mine stone or ore blocks. The diamond pickaxe can mine all types of blocks, so we'll use it for all the turtles in this book. With the pickaxe equipped, the turtle can call the turtle.dig() function, which I'll explain in the next section, to mine blocks or chop wood.

DESIGNING A TREE-CHOPPING ALGORITHM

Before we write code, let's thoroughly think through what the lumberjack turtle needs to do. By planning ahead of time, you'll spot mistakes in your program early instead of discovering them only after you've written it. As the old carpenter saying goes, "measure twice; cut once." We will be planning the turtle's tree-chopping algorithm. An *algorithm* is a series of steps for a computer to follow to solve a problem.

To chop down a tree, we'll start the turtle at the base, dig, move forward, dig above the turtle, move up, and then repeat the last two steps for the whole tree. When the turtle is done, it will move back to the ground so it can be picked up. Figures 6-2 to 6-6 show this entire process.

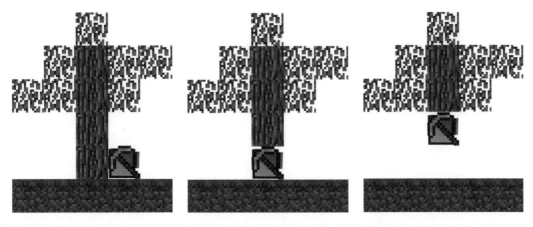

Figure 6-2: The turtle starts at the bottom of the tree, facing the bottom wood block.

Figure 6-3: The turtle chops the bottom wood block, and then moves forward so it is under the tree.

Figure 6-4: The turtle chops upward, and then moves up one space.

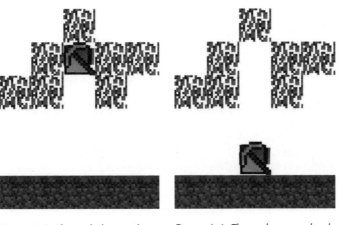

Figure 6-5: The turtle keeps chopping up until there are no more wood blocks above it.

Figure 6-6: The turtle moves back down to the ground so the player can pick it up. The leaves will decompose.

We'll need to use the `turtle.forward()` and `turtle.up()` functions to move the turtle. We'll also use the `turtle.dig()` function, which makes the turtle dig (that is, mine) the block in front of it, as well as the `turtle.digUp()` function, which digs the block above the turtle.

Trees in Minecraft come in all sorts of heights, so the last thing you want to do is write a program that hardcodes the height of the tree the turtle can cut down. *Hardcoding* means to write a program with a limited, fixed solution. Hardcoded programs can't handle different situations without the programmer rewriting the code. So you *don't* want to write code like this:

```
turtle.digUp()
turtle.up()
turtle.digUp()
turtle.up()
turtle.digUp()
turtle.up()
turtle.digUp()
```

Although this program might be easy to understand, the turtle can only chop down trees that are *exactly* four blocks tall. If you want the turtle to chop down a different-sized tree, you'll have to rewrite the code, which is not ideal.

Instead, let's design an algorithm for chopping down trees of any size. For example, we can use these steps for the tree-chopping algorithm:

1. Start on the ground at the base of the tree, facing the tree.

2. Chop the bottom wood block in front of the turtle.

3. Move underneath the tree.

4. Chop wood blocks above the turtle, and move up after each chop until there is no more wood above.

5. Move down until the turtle is back on the ground.

6. Stop.

This algorithm allows the turtle to chop down trees of any height. Now it'll be easy to harvest wood! You'll implement this algorithm in the `choptree` program.

WRITING THE CHOPTREE PROGRAM

Run the text editor by entering `edit choptree` at the command shell. In the text editor, enter the following lines of code. Remember not to type the line numbers because they're only used for reference.

choptree
```
1. --[[Tree Chopping program by Al Sweigart
2. Chops down the tree in front of turtle.]]
3.
4. if not turtle.detect() then
5.   error('Could not find tree!')
6. end
```

```
 7.
 8. print('Chopping tree...')
 9.
10. if not turtle.dig() then  -- chop base of tree
11.   error('Turtle needs a digging tool!')
12. end
13.
14. turtle.forward()  -- move under tree
15. while turtle.compareUp() do
16.   -- keep chopping until no more wood
17.   turtle.digUp()
18.   turtle.up()
19. end
20.
21. -- move back down to ground
22. while not turtle.detectDown() do
23.   turtle.down()
24. end
25.
26. print('Done chopping tree.')
```

After you've entered all of these instructions, save the choptree program.

RUNNING THE CHOPTREE PROGRAM

Use a pickaxe to mine the turtle and put it in your inventory. Find a tree in the Minecraft world, and place the turtle so it's facing the bottommost wood block of the tree, as in Figure 6-7.

Figure 6-7: Place the turtle facing the bottommost wood block of a tree.

Right-click the turtle to open its GUI and make sure that the turtle has fuel and that its current slot is empty so the wood blocks it chops can go there. Then run the choptree program and watch it harvest all the wood from the tree. When the turtle is done harvesting the wood, it will come back to the ground, where you can mine it back into your inventory.

If you get errors when running this program, carefully compare your code to the code in this book to find any typos. If you still cannot fix your program, delete the file by running delete choptree and then download it by running pastebin get 8NgPXXxN choptree.

DETECTING BLOCKS WITH THE TURTLE DETECTION FUNCTIONS

Let's review the source code for the choptree program line by line. The turtle first needs to check whether a tree is in front of it.

choptree
```
1. --[[Tree Chopping program by Al Sweigart
2. Chops down the tree in front of turtle.]]
3.
4. if not turtle.detect() then
```

The turtle.detect() function returns true if something is in front of the turtle and false if there is empty air. The function also returns false if water or lava is in front of the turtle because the turtle can move through these kinds of blocks.

Just like there are turtle.digUp() and turtle.digDown() functions in ComputerCraft, the turtle.detectUp() and turtle.detectDown() functions can detect blocks above and below the turtle, respectively. Although the turtle.detect() function can detect whether a solid block is in front of the turtle, it can't detect what kind of block it is. The program relies on the user to set up the turtle correctly in front of a tree.

The not in front of turtle.detect() on line 4 is a Boolean operator, which we will learn about next.

THE NOT BOOLEAN OPERATOR

The not Boolean operator only operates on one Boolean value and works by evaluating an expression to the opposite value. So not true is false and not false is true. Enter the following into the Lua shell:

```
lua> not true
false
lua> not false
true
lua> myAge = 8
lua> not (myAge > 5)
false
```

You can use the not operator on Boolean values like not false or on expressions like not (myAge > 5), which evaluates as follows:

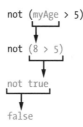

On line 4 of the choptree program, the not operator changes the Boolean value returned by turtle.detect() to its opposite. When there is no block in front of the turtle, turtle.detect() will return false and the not operator will evaluate this as true. The line if not turtle.detect() then can be read as "if the turtle does not detect a block, then run the code." If any block is detected in front of the turtle, the execution enters the code block following the if statement.

There are two other Boolean operators, and and or. We won't use them in the choptree program, but let's take a look at how they work since they will be useful in other programs.

THE AND BOOLEAN OPERATOR

The and Boolean operator compares two Boolean values and evaluates to true if they are *both* true. If either value is false, the entire expression evaluates to false. Enter the following into the Lua shell:

```
lua> true and true
true
lua> true and false
false
lua> false and true
false
lua> false and false
false
```

The order of the values doesn't affect what the expression evaluates to.

You can also use and with more complicated expressions, such as the following:

```
lua> 4 < 5 and 5 < 6
true
lua> myName = 'Al'
lua> theirName = 'Alice'
lua> myName == 'Al' and theirName == 'Bob'
false
```

The expression 4 < 5 and 5 < 6 evaluates like this:

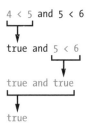

Because both sides of the and operator are true, the expression evaluates to true.

But in myName == 'Al' and theirName == 'Bob', both sides don't evaluate to true:

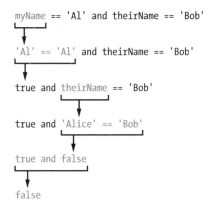

THE OR BOOLEAN OPERATOR

The or Boolean operator compares two Boolean values and evaluates to true if *either* is true. If *both* values are false, the entire expression evaluates to false. Enter the following into the Lua shell:

```
lua> true or true
true
lua> true or false
true
lua> false or true
true
lua> false or false
false
```

Unlike the and operator, only the last expression evaluates to false when using the or operator.

You can also use or with more complicated expressions, like so:

```
lua> 10 > 5 or 'Hello' == 'Hello'
true
lua> myName = 'Al'
lua> myAge = 8
lua> myName == 'Zophie' or myAge < 10
true
lua> myName == 'Zophie' or myAge ~= 8
false
```

The expression myName == 'Zophie' or myAge < 10 evaluates like this:

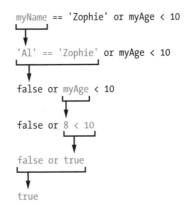

Even though one side of myName == 'Zophie' or myAge < 10 is false, the other side is true, so the entire expression evaluates to true. However, both sides of myName == 'Zophie' or myAge ~= 8 evaluate to false:

```
myName == 'Zophie' or myAge ~= 8
        ↓
'Al' == 'Zophie' or myAge ~= 8
  ↓
false or myAge ~= 8
            ↓
false or 8 ~= 8
           ↓
false or false
  ↓
false
```

This is why myName == 'Zophie' or myAge ~= 8 evaluates to false.

Like the and operator, the or operator will work with expressions that use different data types.

The Boolean operators and, or, and not let you make more sophisticated conditions for your if, elseif, and while statements.

TERMINATING PROGRAMS WITH THE ERROR() FUNCTION

Let's return to the choptree program. If nothing is in front of the turtle when the choptree program runs—that is, if not turtle.detect() on line 4 is true—the program should terminate with an error message. Normally, programs only terminate when they reach the end of the code. However, you can call the error() function with a string argument to terminate the program early and display an error message. When you call the error() function *without* passing a string argument, the program will simply stop without displaying an error message.

We want to show an error message if the turtle isn't facing a block, so we use error() and pass it a string argument on line 5:

choptree

```
4. if not turtle.detect() then
5.    error('Could not find tree!')
6. end
```

If no block is in front of the turtle, then the program stops and prints choptree:5:Could not find tree! to the turtle's GUI. The choptree:5 part is added by Lua to say that line 5 of the choptree program had an error. As a result, the program will stop if there isn't a wood block to chop down in front of the turtle.

MINING BLOCKS WITH THE TURTLE DIGGING FUNCTIONS

If the not turtle.detect() condition on line 4 is false, that is, if the turtle does detect something in front of it, then error() won't be called. Instead, the choptree program will chop the bottom block of the tree using turtle.dig() and then move the turtle under the tree. The wood block will appear in the current slot (or another slot if there are items already in the current slot). Lines 8 through 14 print a message telling the user the program has started, make the turtle chop, and then move the turtle under the tree.

choptree

```
8. print('Chopping tree...')
9.
10. if not turtle.dig() then  -- chop base of tree
11.    error('Turtle needs a digging tool!')
12. end
13.
14. turtle.forward()  -- move under tree
```

Note that the turtle must have a pickaxe or else turtle.dig() won't work and will return false. If this happens, the turtle won't be able to chop down the tree. When the turtle.dig() function returns false, it makes the not turtle.dig() condition true, so line 11 will stop the program and display the error message choptree:11:Turtle needs a digging tool!.

In addition to `turtle.dig()`, the `turtle.digUp()` and `turtle.digDown()` functions will chop or mine the block above or below the turtle, respectively.

COMPARING BLOCKS WITH THE TURTLE COMPARISON FUNCTIONS

The `turtle.compare()` function compares the block that the turtle is facing with the block in the turtle's current slot. If they're the same, `turtle.compare()` returns true. If they're different, `turtle.compare()` returns false. The turtle `.compareUp()` and `turtle.compareDown()` functions do the same thing, except they compare the block above or below the turtle, respectively.

Because the first part of the program chops the bottommost wood block before moving the turtle under the tree, there should be a wood block loaded in the turtle's current slot. We need to check whether the block above the turtle is the same type as the block in its current slot, which is why it is important to make sure the current slot is empty before starting the program. We use `turtle.compareUp()` to do this. The function looks above the turtle instead of in front of it and returns true as long as there is a wood block above the turtle.

choptree

```
15. while turtle.compareUp() do
16.     -- keep chopping until no more wood
17.     turtle.digUp()
18.     turtle.up()
19. end
```

The `while` loop that begins on line 15 uses the return value of turtle `.compareUp()` for its condition. As long as there is wood above the turtle, the program will keep executing the code in the `while` loop. Line 17 digs above the turtle and line 18 moves the turtle up. The loop only stops when turtle `.compareUp()` returns false, which happens when there is no wood above the turtle.

Note that in situations where you might need it, you can use the turtle `.compareDown()` function to compare the block under the turtle.

RETURNING TO THE GROUND

The program execution leaves the `while` loop when no more wood is above the turtle. When the turtle finishes chopping, it should return to the ground.

choptree

```
21. -- move back down to ground
22. while not turtle.detectDown() do
23.     turtle.down()
24. end
25.
26. print('Done chopping tree.')
```

On line 22, we use a `while` loop to check not `turtle.detectDown()`. As long as the turtle doesn't detect a block under it, the condition will return true and call `turtle.down()`. When the loop has ended and the turtle is back on the ground, the program prints `Done chopping tree.` to let the player know that it's time to mine the turtle and pick it up (along with all the chopped wood).

STARTUP PROGRAMS AND THE SHELL.RUN() FUNCTION

We can make this program easier to use by running the choptree program as soon as the turtle is placed in front of a tree. Using a special startup program, we can make the program run whenever the turtle is placed and the GUI is first opened. We'll create the startup program next.

Run the text editor by entering `edit startup` at the command shell. In the text editor, enter the following line of code:

startup

```
shell.run('choptree')
```

The `shell.run()` function will run the string you pass it as though you typed it at the command prompt. In this case, the turtle runs startup when you first open its GUI, and the startup program runs choptree so you don't have to type choptree at the command prompt. The `shell.run()` function returns `true` if it ran the program and returns `false` if it couldn't find the program or if the program stopped because `error()` was called.

BONUS ACTIVITY: GOING DOWN

Create a program that makes the turtle dig a deep hole instead of chopping up a tree. You can do this by making the turtle repeatedly call `turtle.digDown()` and `turtle.down()` using loops. Make the turtle call `turtle.up()` the same number of times it calls `turtle.down()` so it returns back to the surface. You don't want the turtle to get stuck at the bottom of the hole!

WHAT YOU LEARNED

The lumberjack turtle we programmed will speed up the rate that you can harvest wood. If you build multiple lumberjack turtles and load the choptree and startup programs on them, you can have many turtles chopping at once. Set one turtle at a tree, and then while it's mining wood blocks, set another turtle at another tree, and so on. You'll have a huge wood supply in no time!

You can then use the wood that these turtles chop to fuel your turtles. Be sure to craft four planks from each wood block first because wood and planks both provide 15 fuel units.

As big of a help as this lumberjack turtle can be, it still takes a lot of manual work to set it up at the base of each tree. In the next few chapters, you'll learn how to reuse your code and how to make a tree farm by programming turtles to automatically grow and harvest trees.

7

CREATING MODULES TO REUSE YOUR CODE

As your programs become more sophisticated, you might want to reuse code you've already written to save time. Fortunately, you can reuse your code as a *module*, which is a program that contains functions that other programs can call.

In this chapter, you'll learn how to create custom functions and your own module. The turtles will need to run these functions in Chapter 8, so you'll write functions your tree farmer turtles (and the turtles you make in later chapters) will load as a module.

CREATING FUNCTIONS WITH THE FUNCTION STATEMENT

To create your own functions, you use a function statement, which is made up of the function keyword followed by the name of the function and a set of parentheses. All the code following the function statement and prior to an end statement is part of the function.

Let's look at how a function works by writing one. Create a new program by running **edit hellofunction** and entering the following code:

hellofunction

```
1. print('Start of the program.')
2.
3. function hello()
4.    print('Hello, world!')
5. end
6.
7. hello()
8. hello()
9. print('End of the program.')
```

Then run **hellofunction** from the command shell. The output will look like this:

```
> hellofunction
Start of the program.
Hello, world!
Hello, world!
End of the program.
```

Line 1 prints Start of the program. and isn't part of a function. Line 3 creates the hello() function, but notice that the hello() function doesn't run here and the execution skips to line 7 instead.

The code in a function doesn't run when you create the function. It runs only when the function is called. You call a function in the program by using its name followed by a set of parentheses. This syntax tells the program to execute the code contained in the function. We call the hello() function on line 7, which makes the execution move to line 4 where the function was created. Line 4 prints Hello, world!.

When the function call ends, the program returns to the line that originally called the function and continues on. In this case, when the execution reaches the end statement of the hello() function, it returns to line 7 where it was called and then moves to line 8. Line 8 also calls hello(), which makes the execution return to the function on line 4 and print Hello, world! again. Then, when the execution reaches the end of the hello() function, it returns to line 8. Finally, line 9 prints End of the program. and the program terminates.

The `hello()` function is simple, but it isn't any more convenient than writing two `print()` calls. However, as your programs become more complex, organizing your code into functions will become more useful, especially when you begin using arguments.

ARGUMENTS AND PARAMETERS

We can send values to a function when we call the function. These values are known as *arguments.* The arguments are assigned to variables known as *parameters.* The parameters are used inside the function just like variables.

To see how arguments and parameters work, create a new program by running **edit sayhello** and entering the following code. This program tells the turtle to print a message to greet another turtle:

sayhello

```
1. function sayHello(name) -- name is a parameter
2.   print('Hello, ' .. name)
3. end
4.
5. sayHello('Artemisia') -- 'Artemisia' is an argument
6. sayHello('Elisabetta') -- 'Elisabetta' is an argument
```

In this program, the name variable in the sayHello function statement on line 1 is a parameter. The strings 'Artemisia' and 'Elisabetta' on lines 5 and 6 are arguments.

Line 1 creates the sayHello() function, but sayHello() runs only when it's called, so the execution skips to line 5. Line 5 is a function call to the sayHello() function. When we use an argument in a function call like this, we say we are *passing* the argument to the function call. Line 5 passes 'Artemisia' as an argument to sayHello(), which makes the execution move to the sayHello() function on line 2. Then, the name variable, which is the function's parameter, is set to the argument it was passed, which is 'Artemisia'. The name variable is used in the print() function call on line 2, so the program prints Hello, Artemisia.

When the execution reaches the end of the sayHello() function, it returns to line 5 and then moves to line 6. Line 6 calls sayHello() again, but this time passes 'Elisabetta' as an argument, which makes the execution set name to 'Elisabetta'. The execution moves to line 2 and prints Hello, Elisabetta. Then the execution reaches the end of the sayHello() function and returns to line 6. Because there are no more lines of code, the program terminates.

Run the sayhello program on your turtle. It will display the following:

```
> sayhello
Hello, Artemisia
Hello, Elisabetta
```

The sayHello() function will print different strings depending on the argument passed to it.

RETURN VALUES

Function calls evaluate to a *return value*, which you can use like any other value. As a result, you can use function calls in an expression anywhere you would use a value. For example, enter the following into the Lua shell.

```
lua> math.random(1, 6) + 1
5
```

The function call math.random(1, 6) returns a random value from 1 to 6. In this example, that return value is 4, so this expression evaluates to 4 + 1, which then evaluates to the value 5. (You probably got a different number since math.random() is random, after all.)

When creating your own function, you specify the return value using a return statement. A return statement is made up of the return keyword followed by a value or expression. To see how return statements work, create a new program by running **edit givecandy** and entering the following code:

givecandy

```
1. function candiesToGive(name)
2.   if name == 'Al' then
3.     return 10
4.   end
5.
6.   return 2
7. end
8.
9. lavCandy = candiesToGive('Lavinia')
10. alCandy = candiesToGive('Al')
11. print('Lavinia gets ' .. lavCandy .. ' pieces')
12. print('Al gets ' .. alCandy .. ' pieces')
```

The candiesToGive() function returns either the value 10 or 2 depending on what is passed in for its name parameter. When 'Al' is passed to the function, the if statement in the function is true, which makes the execution move to line 3 and return 10. When any other value is passed to the function, the if statement's comparison is false, so the execution skips ahead to line 6, making the function return 2. You can think of arguments as the input to a function and return values as the output.

On line 9, when 'Lavinia' is passed to candiesToGive(), the function returns 2, which means the variable lavCandy is assigned to 2. On line 10, alCandy is assigned to the value 10, which is returned by candiesToGive() when 'Al' is passed as an argument. The variables lavCandy and alCandy can be used in a print() function call, as on lines 11 and 12, because they both store return values.

When you run this program, the output looks like this:

```
> givecandy
Lavinia gets 2 pieces
Al gets 10 pieces
```

MAKING A MODULE OF FUNCTIONS

Instead of typing functions into every program that uses them, you can just type functions into a module once, and then every program that loads the module can use them. This is called *code reuse*.

You create modules with the edit program the same way you create programs, and then you can import the modules into other programs. In this chapter, you'll learn how to create a module, and in the next chapter, you'll learn how to use modules in other programs. We'll create the hare module now (as in the fable "The Tortoise and the Hare") and use it to give all our turtles some handy utility functions.

Create the hare module by running **edit hare** in the command shell and entering the following code:

hare

```
1. --[[Function Module program by Al Sweigart
2. Provides useful utility functions.]]
3.
4. -- selectItem() selects the inventory
5. -- slot with the named item, returns
6. -- true if found and false if not
7. function selectItem(name)
8.    -- check all inventory slots
9.    local item
10.   for slot = 1, 16 do
11.     item = turtle.getItemDetail(slot)
12.     if item ~= nil and item['name'] == name then
13.       turtle.select(slot)
14.       return true
15.     end
16.   end
17.
18.   return false  -- couldn't find item
19. end
20.
21.
22. -- selectEmptySlot() selects inventory
23. -- slot that is empty, returns true if
24. -- found, false if no empty spaces
25. function selectEmptySlot()
26
27.   -- loop through all slots
28.   for slot = 1, 16 do
29.     if turtle.getItemCount(slot) == 0 then
30.       turtle.select(slot)
31.       return true
32.     end
33.   end
34.   return false -- couldn't find empty space
35. end
```

This module is 35 lines long, but you only have to type it once. Without this module, you would have to type this code in every program you want to use it in. Modules save you a lot of time! In the next section, we'll experiment with the hare module's functions in the Lua shell.

If you get errors when running this program, carefully compare your code to the code in this book to find any typos. If you still cannot fix your program, delete the file by running delete hare and then download it by running pastebin get wwzvaKuW hare. (Note that the hare module you download from pastebin contains all the functions added to it in the book, not just the ones added in this chapter.)

LOADING A MODULE WITH THE OS.LOADAPI() FUNCTION

The hare module contains two functions: selectItem() and selectEmptySlot(). The selectItem() function selects an inventory slot containing a given item, and the selectEmptySlot() function selects the first inventory slot it can find that has nothing in it. Both functions are useful when you're working with a turtle's inventory.

Lua's built-in modules (such as the math or os modules) are automatically loaded for all turtle programs, but you need to load the modules you create by calling the os.loadAPI() function. Note that ComputerCraft also calls modules *application programming interfaces (APIs)*. To use os.loadAPI(), pass the name of the module you want to load as a string value. For example, you'll need to run os.loadAPI('hare') to use the hare module's functions in the rest of your program.

The os.loadAPI() function makes the program's functions available to the calling program. The function returns true if the module was found and run. It returns false if the module doesn't exist—for example, if you made a typo, such as os.loadAPI('har'). In the next section, you'll load the hare module and call some of its functions.

EXPERIMENTING WITH THE HARE MODULE

To see how the selectItem() function works, open the turtle's GUI and put oak logs and several other items in the turtle's inventory, as shown in Figure 7-1.

Then, open the Lua shell and enter the following code to select the slot containing the logs:

```
lua> os.loadAPI('hare')
true
lua> hare.selectItem('minecraft:log')
true
```

The first line of code loads the hare module, and the second line of code selects wooden log blocks in the turtle's inventory by passing the string 'minecraft:log' to selectItem().

Figure 7-1: The turtle's GUI contains oak logs and various items with slot 1 as the current slot.

The 'minecraft:log' string is the Minecraft name ID for oak logs. A *name ID* is a unique string beginning with 'minecraft:' that Minecraft uses to identify blocks and inventory items. You can find a list of name IDs in "List of Block Name IDs" on page 219. In "Getting Item Details from a Slot" on page 80, you'll learn how to get an item's name ID with the turtle.getItemDetail() function instead of having to look it up.

When you look at the turtle's inventory, notice that the wooden log block is currently selected, as shown in Figure 7-2. The hare.selectItem() function can find and select the log no matter which inventory slot it's in. Try moving the log to a different slot and running hare.selectItem('minecraft:log') again. The slot the log is in will be selected again, as indicated by the thick border around the slot.

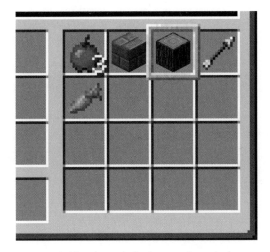

Figure 7-2: The slot with the log is selected after running hare.selectItem('minecraft:log').

The selectEmptySlot() function selects the first inventory slot it can find that has nothing in it. This function is useful when you're about to mine blocks, because you need an empty slot to store the mined blocks in. In the Lua shell, run the following code:

```
lua> os.loadAPI('hare')
true
lua> hare.selectEmptySlot()
true
```

After calling hare.selectEmptySlot(), the first empty slot will be selected, as shown in Figure 7-3.

Figure 7-3: The first empty slot is selected after calling hare.selectEmptySlot().

The tree-farming program in Chapter 8 will use the two functions selectItem() and selectEmptySlot(), but they could be useful in many turtle programs. Let's look at the code behind them.

LOOKING AT THE TURTLE'S INVENTORY

The first part of the hare module contains comments for the program and additional comments that explain what the selectItem() function does.

hare
```
1. --[[Function Module program by Al Sweigart
2. Provides useful utility functions.]]
3.
4. -- selectItem() selects the inventory
5. -- slot with the named item, returns
6. -- true if found and false if not
7. function selectItem(name)
```

The function statement for the selectItem() function is on line 7. Remember that the code in the block that follows the function statement is executed whenever the function is *called*. The code in the block doesn't run when the function statement is first encountered. To understand the function code in selectItem(), you first need to learn about certain functions that are used to look at the turtle's inventory.

Each turtle has an inventory of 16 slots, numbered as shown in Figure 7-4.

Turtles have three built-in functions that allow you to interact with the turtle's inventory using the slot numbers. These functions are called turtle.select(), turtle.getItemCount(), and turtle.getItemDetail(). Let's look at how these functions work in more detail.

Figure 7-4: The numbered inventory slots of a turtle

SELECTING AN INVENTORY SLOT

You can change the current slot using the turtle.select() function by passing the number of the slot you want to select to the function. See the slot numbers shown in Figure 7-4. Enter the following lines into the Lua shell to see how this function works:

```
lua> turtle.select(2)
true
lua> turtle.select(16)
true
```

After you call the function, notice the thick border that indicates the current slot change. Many other turtle functions use the current slot, so knowing how to change it in your programs is useful when you need to interact with a specific slot or item in a slot.

COUNTING THE NUMBER OF ITEMS IN A SLOT

If you want to know how many items are in an inventory slot, call the turtle.getItemCount() function and pass it a slot number. Enter the following lines into the Lua shell:

```
lua> turtle.getItemCount(1)
1
lua> turtle.getItemCount(16)
0
```

If you don't pass any argument to turtle.getItemCount(), the function checks the currently selected slot. This function is straightforward and returns the number of items in an inventory slot, but it doesn't tell you anything about what is inside the inventory slot. To learn the details about what is stored in the slot, you need to use the turtle.getItemDetail() function.

GETTING ITEM DETAILS FROM A SLOT

You can detect the specifics of what is in the turtle's inventory by calling the turtle.getItemDetail() function and passing the function the slot number you want to check. Put a wooden log inside inventory slot 1, and then enter the following code into the Lua shell:

```
lua> turtle.getItemDetail(1)
{
  count = 1,
  name = "minecraft:log",
  damage = 0,
}
```

The value that turtle.getItemDetail() returns indicates that one log is in inventory slot 1. If nothing is in that inventory slot, turtle.getItemDetail() returns nil. If you don't pass any arguments to turtle.getItemDetail(), it returns information about the currently selected slot.

The returned value looks completely different from the other values you've seen so far because it's a table value.

THE TABLE DATA TYPE

Table values can hold multiple values. Similar to how strings begin and end with quotes, values of the table data type begin and end with braces, { }. The values that a table value holds are organized in *key-value pairs*, which are listed and separated by commas. Enter the following line into the Lua shell to create a new table value and see what these pairs look like:

```
lua> myStuff = {logs=5, stone=4, arrows=10}
```

This line assigns the table value {logs=5, stone=4, arrows=10} to the variable myStuff. The three number values in this table—5, 4, and 10—are the *value* part of the key-value pairs. They can be identified by their respective keys: 'logs', 'stone', and 'arrows'. Together, a key and a value form a key-value pair, such as logs=5, with the key first, followed by an equal sign (=), and then followed by the value. Keys and values can be almost any data type, so a key can be an integer or a value can be a string. The only exception is that a table key cannot be the nil value.

To access the individual values inside the table, enter the variable myStuff followed by the key inside square brackets, [ ]. This statement will evaluate to the value in the table associated with that key. For example, enter the following into the Lua shell to access a value from the table we created earlier:

```
lua> myStuff['logs']
5
lua> 'I have ' .. myStuff['stone'] .. ' stone.'
I have 4 stone.
lua> 'I need ' .. (12 - myStuff['arrows']) .. ' more arrows to have a dozen.'
I need 2 more arrows to have a dozen.
```

The first line of code evaluates to the value associated with `'logs'`, which is the number 5. Because the expression evaluates to a value, you can use it anywhere you would normally use a value, such as when concatenating strings or when doing math (if the value is a number).

EXAMINING THE TABLE RETURNED BY THE TURTLE.GETITEMDETAIL() FUNCTION

Let's look at the `turtle.getItemDetail()` function again. Put one wood log in inventory slot 1, and then enter the following into the Lua shell:

```
lua> item = turtle.getItemDetail(1)
lua> item['name']
minecraft:log
lua> item['count']
1
```

When you enter `item['name']`, you get the value at the key name in the table, which is `minecraft:log`. You can retrieve other values, such as the value associated with the key count, too. Now you have a way to get the turtle's inventory information as string and number values! Notice that if `turtle.getItemDetail()` returns `nil` because nothing is in that inventory slot, trying to use the square brackets will result in an error:

```
lua> item = turtle.getItemDetail(16)
lua> item['name']
lua:1: attempt to index ? (a nil value)
```

To prevent this error from happening in your programs, make sure `item` is not set to `nil` by using an `if` statement. Although we won't use this code in this chapter's program, if you need to do this in a future program, you can use the following code:

```
local item = turtle.getItemDetail(16)
if item ~= nil then
    print(item['name'])
end
```

With this code, `item['name']` runs only if `item` is not equal (`~=`) to nil.

GLOBAL AND LOCAL SCOPE

The `selectItem()` function will find an item in the turtle's inventory that corresponds to the string passed to the function's name parameter. This function first declares a local variable named `item` on line 9. This local variable only exists inside the `selectItem()` function and cannot be used elsewhere in the program.

```
7. function selectItem(name)
8.    -- check all inventory slots
9.    local item
```

You've already learned about the local keyword in "The Boolean Data Type" on page 49, but you haven't yet learned about scope. A *scope* is a part of the program where a variable is visible, and local variables exist only inside one scope. Lua has two types of scopes: global and local.

Variables declared in the *global scope* are declared outside of any function and are visible in all parts of the program. This can cause problems if you accidentally reuse a variable name because the program will use any previously stored values in the variable or will allow functions to overwrite a variable with a new value. To address this issue, you can make variables in *local scopes*, which you create every time you make a function. When a variable is declared local to a function, it will exist only in that function's local scope and will cease to exist once the function returns.

By using local variables, you can have two variables with the same name as long as they exist in different scopes. Because you'll add more functions to the hare module in the future, we've declared item as local to the selectItem() function. Unless you need a variable that can be accessed throughout the entire program, it's best to declare variables as local in every function to avoid future problems.

Variables used in a for loop, such as the i variable in for i = 1, 4 do, are local to that for loop. These variables will not exist outside the for loop, just like the variables local to a function will not exist outside the function.

FINDING AN ITEM WITH A FOR LOOP

After we've set up our variables, the program creates a variable named slot that is local to the for loop on line 10.

```
10.    for slot = 1, 16 do
11.      item = turtle.getItemDetail(slot)
12.      if item ~= nil and item['name'] == name then
13.        turtle.select(slot)
14.        return true
15.      end
16.    end
17.
18.    return false  -- couldn't find item
19. end
```

The slot variable in for slot = 1, 16 do will not exist after the loop's end statement. It is local to the for loop. The for loop sets slot to each of the values between 1 and 16. Inside this for loop, line 11 gets the table value of the inventory item at `slot` and stores the value in `item`. Line 12 checks that `item` isn't `nil` and also checks whether the item's name matches the `name` parameter. If the names match, the program has found the item and selects that slot. Line 14 returns `true` to tell the code that `selectItem()` has selected the item.

The end statement on line 15 closes the `if` statement, and the end statement on line 16 closes the `for` loop statement. If the execution completes all iterations of the `for` loop and hasn't found an item with a matching name, the function returns `false` on line 18. Finally, the end statement on line 19 closes the `function` statement.

SELECTING AN EMPTY INVENTORY SLOT

The `selectEmptySlot()` function tries to find an empty inventory slot. If it finds one, it selects the slot using `turtle.select()` and returns `true`. If the turtle's inventory is completely full, the function will return `false`. Like the `selectItem()` function, `selectEmptySlot()` has a `for` loop that checks inventory slots 1 to 16. The `for` loop in this function also declares the variable `slot` on line 28, which it can do because the `slot` variable defined on line 10 and this `slot` variable are in different local scopes.

hare
```
25. function selectEmptySlot()
26.
27.    -- loop through all slots
28.    for slot = 1, 16 do
29.      if turtle.getItemCount(slot) == 0 then
30.        turtle.select(slot)
31.        return true
32.      end
33.    end
34.    return false -- couldn't find empty space
35. end
```

Inside the loop, line 29 calls `turtle.getItemCount()` to check whether the number of items in the slot currently being checked is 0. When line 29 finds the first empty inventory slot, line 30 selects this slot and line 31 returns `true`.

If the execution makes it through all iterations of the `for` loop without finding any empty inventory slots, line 34 returns `false`.

BONUS ACTIVITY: DANCE MOVE MODULE

Try creating a new module of dance moves that the turtle can perform. You can write functions for performing hops, spins, and moonwalking (walking backward).

WHAT YOU LEARNED

In this chapter, you learned how to create modules and your own functions with `function` statements. Functions can have parameters, which are passed arguments as input. Functions can also return a value to the code that called the function.

Functions create a new local scope every time they're called. When the function returns, the scope is destroyed along with all the variables in it, which means different variables can have the same name as long as they're in different scopes. A `for` loop's variable also exists in its own local scope inside the loop's block. The functions in your `hare` module call other ComputerCraft functions: `turtle.select()`, `turtle.getItemDetail()`, and `turtle.getItemCount()`.

You can place the functions you make inside modules to let other programs use them. Creating your own functions and modules is a programming technique that enables you to make more sophisticated turtle programs. In the Chapter 8, you'll use the `hare` module to create a tree farm to automatically harvest wood logs.

8

RUNNING AN AUTOMATED TREE FARM

In Chapter 6, we programmed a turtle to chop down a tree, but the player still has to manually place the turtle in front of a tree before the program can run. Placing a turtle in front of each tree you want to chop down isn't much more efficient than harvesting a tree yourself. We can remove this manual step and fully automate the lumber-milling process by also programming the turtle to plant and grow saplings. As a result, the turtle can plant a sapling, harvest it when it becomes a tree, then plant a new sapling, and repeat the process without any human intervention! To do this, we'll write a program called farmtrees. You can set up multiple turtles to grow trees, as shown in Figure 8-1.

Figure 8-1: An automated tree farm tended by turtles, with each turtle running the farmtrees program

We'll reuse code we've already written in the hare module (Chapter 7) and choptree program (Chapter 6) to harvest the wood, so there's no need to rewrite all that code!

DESIGNING A TREE-FARMING PROGRAM

Instead of moving the turtle to each tree, we'll set up the turtle to stay in one place. The turtle will plant and grow saplings using bone meal to speed up the sapling's growth. Then, once the sapling has grown into a tree, the turtle will harvest it and place the harvested wood into a chest behind the turtle.

Here are the steps of the tree-farming program in detail:

1. Check to make sure the hare module and choptree program exist.
2. Select tree saplings in the turtle's inventory. Quit the program if it doesn't have any.
3. Plant the sapling.
4. Repeatedly use bone meal on the planted sapling until it grows.
5. Run the choptree program.
6. Place the harvested wood in a chest behind the turtle.
7. Repeat the entire process.

The turtle will repeat the process until it runs out of tree saplings or bone meal. Now that we know what the code should do, let's write the program.

WRITING THE FARMTREES PROGRAM

Run the text editor by entering **edit farmtrees** at the command shell. In the text editor, enter the following lines of code. Remember not to type the line numbers because they're only used for reference.

farmtrees

```
1. --[[Tree Farming program by Al Sweigart
2. Plants tree then cuts it down.]]
3.
4. os.loadAPI('hare')  -- load the hare module
5.
6. local blockExists, item
7. local logCount = 0
8.
9. -- check if choptree program exists
10. if not fs.exists('choptree') then
11.   error('You must install choptree program first.')
12. end
13.
14. while true do
15.   -- check inventory for saplings
16.   if not hare.selectItem('minecraft:sapling') then
17.     error('Out of saplings.')
18.   end
19.
20.   print('Planting...')
21.   turtle.place()  -- plant sapling
22.
23.   -- loop until a tree has grown
24.   while true do
25.     blockExists, item = turtle.inspect()
26.     if blockExists and item['name'] == 'minecraft:sapling' then
27.       -- "dye" is the name ID for bone meal
28.       if not hare.selectItem('minecraft:dye') then
29.         error('Out of bone meal.')
30.       end
31.
32.       print('Using bone meal...')
33.       turtle.place()  -- use bone meal
34.     else
35.       break  -- tree has grown
36.     end
37.   end
38.
39.   hare.selectEmptySlot()
40.   shell.run('choptree')  -- run choptree
41.
42.   -- move to and face chest
43.   turtle.back()
44.   turtle.turnLeft()
45.   turtle.turnLeft()
46.
```

```
47.    -- put logs into chest
48.    while hare.selectItem('minecraft:log') do
49.      logCount = logCount + turtle.getItemCount()
50.      print('Total logs: ' .. logCount)
51.      turtle.drop()
52.    end
53.
54.    -- face planting spot
55.    turtle.turnLeft()
56.    turtle.turnLeft()
57. end
```

After you've entered all of the code, press the CTRL key, make sure **[Save]** is selected, and press ENTER. Then quit the editor by pressing CTRL, selecting **[Exit]**, and then pressing ENTER.

RUNNING THE FARMTREES PROGRAM

Before you run the farmtrees program, you need do some setup. First, ensure that a chest is directly behind the turtle and that saplings and bone meal are in the turtle's inventory, as shown in Figure 8-2.

Figure 8-2: Place a chest behind the turtle and put saplings and bone meal in the turtle's inventory.

You can craft bone meal from the bones dropped when you defeat skeletons. Use the recipe shown in Figure 8-3 to craft bone meal.

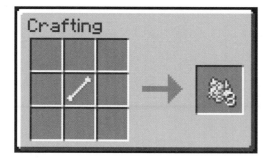

Figure 8-3: Crafting three bone meal from one bone

Second, make sure you've left one inventory slot empty to store the wood that the turtle will harvest.

When you're finished with all the preparations for the program, run farmtrees. You should see the turtle plant a tree sapling and then chop down the sapling once it grows into a tree. Next, the turtle will return to the ground and face the chest to drop off the wood it collected. Then the turtle will turn around to face its original direction and repeat the process.

If you get errors when running this program, carefully compare your code to the code in this book to find any typos. If you still cannot fix your program, delete the file by running delete farmtrees and then download it by running pastebin get v5h8AgGs farmtrees.

TREE TYPES IN MINECRAFT

Although Minecraft has many different types of trees, each with their own kind of sapling, certain trees are better to use in farmtrees than others because the turtle will harvest one column of a tree, moving straight up. If a tree branches out, the turtle will stop harvesting very quickly because it won't follow the tree's curve. Therefore, the best trees to use have tall, narrow trunks like the oak, spruce, birch, and jungle trees shown in Figure 8-4. Acacia trees branch out too much to be useful, and dark oak trees require planting saplings in a 2 × 2 area, which means they take up a lot of room.

Figure 8-4: From left to right: oak, spruce, birch, and jungle trees

When we call hare.selectItem() on line 16, all the saplings will have the name 'minecraft:sapling', so when you put saplings into the turtle's inventory for it to farm, be sure they are oak, spruce, birch, or jungle saplings.

CHUNK LOADING IN MINECRAFT

For the `farmtrees` program, you don't need to supervise the turtle while it's harvesting trees, but you shouldn't wander too far from the turtle because of how the Minecraft world works. Minecraft's world is effectively infinite because it generates parts of the world as you move into areas. However, because it would take too much of the computer's memory to load the entire world all the time, Minecraft loads only the areas near the player. In Minecraft, the map is divided into 16-block by 16-block areas called *chunks* that load from the bottom to the top of the game world. As the player moves toward other chunks, the chunks are loaded into the computer's memory from the hard drive and the chunks farthest from the player are unloaded.

Chunks are important to turtle programming because turtles will shut down if the chunk they're in unloads itself. For example, on my computer, turtles shut down if I'm about 400 to 450 blocks away from them. Also, if your **Render Distance** option (found under **Options ▸ Video Settings**) is set to a lower number, the turtles will unload much sooner. If you set up several tree-farming turtles and move somewhere far away to mine, they might stop working. It's best to keep turtles nearby while their programs are running and to fit as many as you can into a small area.

Now that you know all the details on how to use the `farmtrees` program, let's look at each part of its code.

LOADING MODULES WITH THE OS.LOADAPI() FUNCTION

After the comments that describe the program in lines 1 and 2, line 4 loads the hare module that you created in Chapter 7.

farmtrees

```
1. --[[Tree Farming program by Al Sweigart
2. Plants tree then cuts it down.]]
3.
4. os.loadAPI('hare')  -- load the hare module
5.
6. local blockExists, item
7. local logCount = 0
```

To allow the program to call the `hare.selectEmptySlot()` and `hare.selectItem()` functions, which were explained in Chapter 7, your program must first call the `os.loadAPI()` function and pass the string `'hare'` to load the hare module.

Lines 6 and 7 declare variables that the program will use to make them easy to find. The `blockExists` and `item` variables store values later in the program when the turtle checks whether the sapling it planted has grown into a tree. The `logCount` variable keeps track of how many wooden log blocks the turtle has harvested, which is `0` when the program runs for the first time.

CHECKING FOR FILES WITH THE FS.EXISTS() FUNCTION

Before the program starts farming trees, it checks that the choptree program exists on the turtle. Otherwise, you'll get an error when the turtle tries to run the farmtrees program.

farmtrees

```
 9. -- check if choptree program exists
10. if not fs.exists('choptree') then
11.   error('You must install choptree program first.')
12. end
```

You can check for the existence of the choptree program using the fs.exists() function, which takes a filename and returns true if a file with that name exists and false if it does not. If the choptree program doesn't exist, line 11 terminates the program and displays the error message You must install choptree program first.

SELECTING SAPLINGS IN THE TURTLE'S INVENTORY

Line 14 begins the program's while loop, which plants saplings and harvests wood. Every time the program finishes harvesting the wood from the tree it planted, it loops back to line 14 to repeat the process. Because the while loop's condition is always true, it is an infinite loop that doesn't stop until the program terminates with an error() call or break statement (which I explain in "Breaking Out of Loops with break Statements" on page 94).

Inside the while loop, the program first checks the turtle's inventory for saplings.

farmtrees

```
14. while true do
15.   -- check inventory for saplings
16.   if not hare.selectItem('minecraft:sapling') then
17.     error('Out of saplings.')
18.   end
```

Line 16 uses the hare module's selectItem() function to select an inventory slot that contains a tree sapling. If no saplings are in the turtle's inventory, this function returns false. In that case, line 17 terminates the program by calling error() and displaying the error message Out of saplings.

PLANTING A TREE

If the execution passes the sapling check, line 20 displays a status update that the turtle is about to plant a sapling. Line 21 calls the turtle.place() function to do the planting.

farmtrees

```
20.   print('Planting...')
21.   turtle.place() -- plant sapling
```

The turtle.place() function places the block in the current slot in front of the turtle. This function works for saplings as well as planks, stone bricks, or any other block that the player can place in the world. Recall that line 16 selected the inventory slot with saplings, so the turtle.place() function places a sapling. Figure 8-5 shows the sapling after it has been planted in front of the turtle.

Figure 8-5: A sapling planted by the turtle

NOTE   *In situations where you might need them, you can also use the* turtle.placeUp() *and* turtle.placeDown() *functions to place blocks above and below the turtle. These functions return* true *if the placement is successful. If a block is already there or something else prevents the placement of the block, these functions return* false.

INSPECTING BLOCKS AND WAITING FOR THE TREE TO GROW

After planting the sapling, the execution enters another while loop that is inside the while loop on line 14. This inner while loop begins on line 24. Inside this loop, the program inspects the block in front of the turtle using the turtle.inspect() function, which is similar to turtle.detect() except turtle.detect() only returns true or false if a block is present, whereas turtle.inspect() returns a table value with details about what kind of block is in front of the turtle.

farmtrees
```
23.    -- loop until a tree has grown
24.    while true do
25.       blockExists, item = turtle.inspect()
```

The turtle.inspect() function returns two values, which are stored in the blockExists and item variables that were declared at the start of the program. The first returned value (stored in blockExists) is a Boolean true if a block is in front of the turtle or false if no block is in front of the turtle. The second returned value (stored in item) is a table value with information about the block. If no block is in front of the turtle, this second returned value will be nil.

You can find the name of any item by running turtle.inspect() in the Lua shell while the block is in front of the turtle. For example, if a sapling is in front of a turtle and you run the command, you would see this:

```
lua> turtle.inspect()
true
{
  state = {
    type = "oak",
    stage = 0,
  },
  name = "minecraft:sapling",
  metadata = 0,
}
```

The if statement on line 26 checks that a block in front of the turtle exists and that it is a sapling. If it is, then lines 28 to 33 will repeatedly attempt to use bone meal on the sapling to speed its growth into a tree.

farmtrees
```
26.    if blockExists and item['name'] == 'minecraft:sapling' then
27.        -- "dye" is the name ID for bone meal
28.        if not hare.selectItem('minecraft:dye') then
29.          error('Out of bone meal.')
30.        end
```

Line 28 checks the turtle's inventory for bone meal. The name of bone meal items in Minecraft is 'minecraft:dye'. Similar to how the different tree saplings have the same 'minecraft:sapling' name, bone meal shares the name ID 'minecraft:dye' with other types of items.

If no bone meal is in the turtle's inventory, then hare.selectItem('minecraft :dye') returns false and line 29 terminates the program with the error message Out of bone meal.

Otherwise, the execution continues to line 32, where the program prints a message to tell the user what the turtle is doing and then uses the bone meal on the sapling by placing it in front of the turtle.

farmtrees
```
32.        print('Using bone meal...')
33.        turtle.place()  -- use bone meal
```

The execution skips the else statement on line 34 because the condition wasn't false, and there are no further lines in the while loop. After using the bone meal, the execution loops back to line 24 where it repeats the check for a sapling in front of the turtle.

BREAKING OUT OF LOOPS WITH BREAK STATEMENTS

If the condition on line 26 is false, then there is no sapling detected in front of the turtle, and the execution moves to the block after the else statement on line 34. The sapling will be gone because it has grown into a tree and a wood block is now in front of the turtle. When line 35 runs, the break statement causes the execution to exit the while loop that started on line 24.

farmtrees

```
34.     else
35.        break  -- tree has grown
36.     end
37.  end
```

The break statement consists of just the break keyword. A break statement causes the execution to immediately exit a loop and move past it without rechecking the while loop's condition. The break statement on line 35 causes the execution to move to the first line outside the loop, which is line 39.

Line 36 ends the else statement's code block, and line 37 ends the while statement's code block.

RUNNING OTHER PROGRAMS WITH THE SHELL.RUN() FUNCTION

The shell.run() function lets your program execute commands the same way you do at the command shell. The farmtrees program will use this function to run the choptree program.

farmtrees

```
39.  hare.selectEmptySlot()
40.  shell.run('choptree')  -- run choptree
```

Line 39 calls the hare module's selectEmptySlot() function to ensure that the wood blocks the turtle mines will go into an empty inventory slot. (Otherwise, the choptree program won't work.) Then, line 40 runs the choptree program by calling shell.run() and passing the string 'choptree'.

The string passed to shell.run() is the same text you would enter into the command shell. Calling shell.run('choptree') in a program does the same thing as running the choptree program in the command shell.

This is how your program can run other programs. When the choptree program terminates, the execution will continue on from line 40.

HANDLING ITEMS WITH THE TURTLE'S DROP FUNCTIONS

At the end of the choptree program, the turtle will have descended to the ground where the sapling was originally planted. It then moves back one space to return to its original position and turns left twice to face the chest, ready to drop the wood.

```
42.   -- move to and face chest
43.   turtle.back()
44.   turtle.turnLeft()
45.   turtle.turnLeft()
```

The turtle.drop() function makes the turtle drop all the items in the current inventory slot into the chest that it's facing (or on the ground if no chest has been added). If you pass a number to the turtle.drop() function, you can drop a certain number of items in the current slot instead of all of them. For example, the following Lua shell example will drop only one item:

```
lua> turtle.drop(1)
```

NOTE *In situations where you might need them, you can also use the* turtle.dropUp() *and* turtle.dropDown() *functions to drop items above and below the turtle instead of in front of it.*

The while loop continues to select wood blocks as long as they exist in the turtle's inventory. Inside the loop, the code keeps count of the number of logs as they're dropped into the chest.

```
47.   -- put logs into chest
48.   while hare.selectItem('minecraft:log') do
49.     logCount = logCount + turtle.getItemCount()
50.     print('Total logs: ' .. logCount)
51.     turtle.drop()
52.   end
```

The hare.selectItem() function call on line 48 returns true as long as it can find an item with the name ID 'minecraft:log', meaning that the while loop will keep looping as long as wood blocks are in the turtle's inventory. The turtle.getItemCount() call returns the number of logs in the current slot. This count is added to the number in logCount on line 49 to keep track of the total number of wood blocks the turtle places in the chest, and line 50 displays that total number. These logs are then dropped from the turtle's inventory into the chest in front of the turtle using the turtle.drop() function call on line 51.

Lines 55 and 56 make the turtle turn left twice to return to its original position, facing the spot where it planted the sapling. Line 57 marks the end of the while loop that started on line 14, so the execution jumps back to line 14, ready to plant another sapling.

```
54.   -- face planting spot
55.   turtle.turnLeft()
56.   turtle.turnLeft()
57. end
```

Recall that the while loop on line 14 is an infinite loop. The farmtrees program will terminate only if the error() calls on lines 17 or 29 are executed, and that happens if the turtle runs out of either saplings or bone meal, respectively. The player can also terminate the program by holding down CTRL-T. The player can refill the turtle's inventory even while the program is running. As long as the player keeps the turtle stocked with saplings and bone meal, the program will continue to run forever.

REWRITING YOUR CODE FOR WHEN YOU HAVE NO BONE MEAL

As you increase your programming skills, you might think of ideas to improve your programs after they're already written. You can rewrite your programs as much as you like. For example, you might have noticed that the turtles will go through your supply of bone meal faster than you can slay skeletons. Robots don't get bored, so you can reprogram your patient turtle to wait for the tree to grow naturally instead of using bone meal.

Currently, the turtles are programmed to quit if no bone meal is in their inventory. To reprogram them to wait for the sapling to grow into a tree when they run out of bone meal, change line 29 from error('Out of bone meal.') to this:

farmtrees

```
29.        os.sleep(10)
```

The os.sleep() function pauses the program for the number of seconds you pass it. The revised version of line 29 has the turtle sleep for 10 seconds before continuing with the rest of the program. This pause makes the turtle check every 10 seconds to see whether the sapling has grown into a tree.

Another benefit of using os.sleep() instead of just constantly looping is that when os.sleep() is called, Minecraft can stop running the turtle's code and then resume running the code at the end of the pause. Pausing program execution can prevent lag, especially if several turtles are running programs.

BONUS ACTIVITY: LONE TURTLE FARMER

You don't need one turtle per tree for your tree farm. You can set up several tree plots in a line, and then program one turtle to check on each tree every few minutes. Write a program that makes a turtle run the farmtrees program for several plots as in Figure 8-6.

You'll need to modify the farmtrees program so that it only checks whether each tree has grown from a sapling once before moving on to the next plot, instead of checking one tree forever in a loop. This way, you can reuse the code in farmtrees but can create much larger farms.

Figure 8-6: A turtle tending a sapling in one of three plots

WHAT YOU LEARNED

The true power of the farmtrees program is that the program can scale as you add more turtles. If you add 10 turtles, wood production will increase accordingly. This wood is not only useful as building material—it can also be burned in a furnace to turn it into charcoal. Charcoal can be used like coal to fuel turtles, which means these turtles won't need humans to find fuel for them. Better hope they don't rebel!

In this chapter, you learned about the different types of trees in Minecraft. You learned about chunks and how turtles will only continue to run as long as they exist in a loaded chunk in the Minecraft world.

You also learned some additional turtle functions. The fs.exists() function will check if a program exists on the turtle. In farmtrees, the turtle.place() function placed saplings on the ground, but you can also use it to place any kind of block in front of the turtle. The turtle.inspect() function lets the turtle see what block is in front of it. The turtle.drop() function drops items, including into chests. The shell.run() function lets the farmtrees program run other programs, such as the choptree program.

The break statement causes the execution of a program to immediately jump out of a while or for loop. And the os.sleep() function lets you pause your program for a certain number of seconds.

In Chapter 9, we'll expand our automated production to create cobblestone and stone bricks. This stone brick factory will create all the building blocks we need without ever stepping foot into a mine!

BUILDING A COBBLESTONE GENERATOR

The most common blocks you'll find as you mine are stone. They become cobblestone when mined, but you can turn them back into stone by smelting them in a furnace. Then you can craft this stone into stone bricks for your buildings' construction materials.

Whew! That's a lot of work in dangerous, dark mines just to get stone bricks. In this chapter, you'll learn how to create a cobblestone generator that will give you infinite cobblestone to work with, and then you'll create a turtle program to automatically mine and smelt that cobblestone into stone. Safe inside your base, you'll have a production line for an endless amount of stone bricks to build with.

BLUEPRINTS FOR THE COBBLESTONE GENERATOR

Although you can obtain cobblestone by mining it in Minecraft, you can also create it by mixing a stream of water with a stream of lava, which forms a cobblestone block. You can use this knowledge to build a cobblestone generator that performs the same process to create an unlimited number of cobblestone blocks. Turtles can mine this cobblestone forever because their tools don't wear out.

To create a cobblestone generator, follow the blueprint in Figure 9-1. A generator has three layers of blocks. You'll need one type of block to act as an enclosure for holding the water and lava streams. I used glass, but you can use any nonflammable blocks. You'll need to use three iron ingots to craft a bucket, which you'll then fill from a lava pool. Although you can find lava pools on the surface, they're more commonly found deep underground near bedrock. You can draw water from the rivers, ponds, and oceans on the surface.

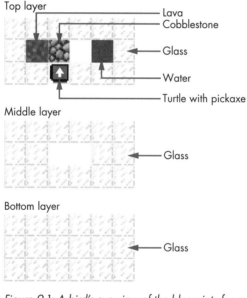

Figure 9-1: A bird's-eye view of the blueprints for a cobblestone generator

When placing the lava and water, *be sure to place the water first.* Otherwise, the water stream will mix directly with the lava block (instead of the lava stream), turning it into obsidian. You don't need to place the cobblestone block in the blueprint. It will form automatically.

Figure 9-2 shows the completed cobblestone generator.

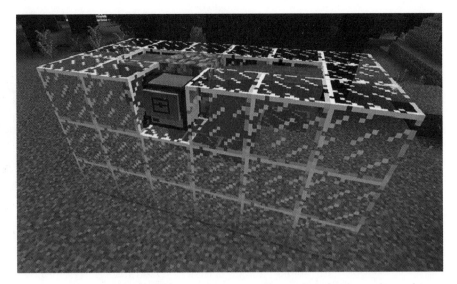

Figure 9-2: The completed cobblestone generator with a turtle in the empty slot on the top layer

Whenever the cobblestone block in the generator is mined, it opens space for the lava to flow into to create a new cobblestone block. You could mine the cobblestone an infinite number of times, but you would wear out a lot of pickaxes. By placing a turtle in the open spot on the top layer facing the cobblestone block, you can have the turtle mine the cobblestone blocks forever. Because the turtle doesn't even need to move, it doesn't use any fuel either!

SETTING UP FURNACES FOR SMELTING THE COBBLESTONE

Even though we now have an infinite supply of cobblestone, we still need to smelt the cobblestone into stone to use it. To do this, we'll create the cobminer program, which will make a turtle mine the cobblestone from the generator and then deposit the mined cobblestone into furnaces to smelt it into stone.

Before you create the cobminer program, you'll need to do some setup. First, you need to extend the cobblestone generator by adding five furnaces to the middle layer behind the turtle, as shown in Figure 9-3.

The turtle running the new cobblestone miner program will mine until it has a full stack of 64 cobblestones. Then it will move backward over the furnaces, dropping the cobblestone into them. The furnaces will smelt the cobblestone into stone. If all the furnaces are full, the turtle will wait five minutes before trying to drop cobblestone into them again. This entire process will repeat forever.

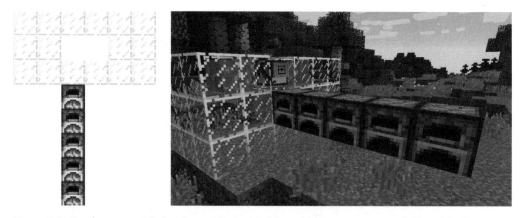

Figure 9-3: Five furnaces added to the middle layer of the cobblestone generator (left) and the furnaces in the game (right)

In Chapter 10, we'll create a brickcrafter program to run a second turtle. The brickcrafter program will pick up the smelted stone from the furnaces and use it to craft stone bricks. The turtle will store these stone brick blocks in a nearby chest for the player.

WRITING THE COBMINER PROGRAM

To write the cobminer program, run **edit cobminer** from the command shell and enter the following code:

cobminer

```
1. --[[Stone Brick Factory program by Al Sweigart
2. Mines cobblestone from a generator, turtle 1 of 2]]
3.
4. os.loadAPI('hare')  -- load the hare module
5. local numToDrop
6. local NUM_FURNACES = 5
7.
8. print('Starting mining program...')
9. while true do
10.    -- mine cobblestone
11.    if turtle.detect() then
12.      print('Cobblestone detected. Mining...')
13.      turtle.dig()  -- mine cobblestone
14.    else
15.      print('No cobblestone. Sleeping...')
16.      os.sleep(0.5)  -- half-second pause
17.    end
18.
19.    -- check for a full stack of cobblestone
20.    hare.selectItem('minecraft:cobblestone')
21.    if turtle.getItemCount() == 64 then
22.      -- check turtle's fuel
23.      if turtle.getFuelLevel() < (2 * NUM_FURNACES) then
24.        error('Turtle needs more fuel!')
25.      end
```

```
26.
27.      -- put cobblestone in furnaces
28.      print('Dropping off cobblestone...')
29.      for furnacesToFill = NUM_FURNACES, 1, -1 do
30.        turtle.back() -- move over furnace
31.        numToDrop = math.floor(turtle.getItemCount() / furnacesToFill)
32.        turtle.dropDown(numToDrop)  -- put cobblestone in furnace
33.      end
34.
35.      -- move back to cobblestone generator
36.      for moves = 1, NUM_FURNACES do
37.        turtle.forward()
38.      end
39.
40.      if turtle.getItemCount() > 0 then
41.        print('All furnaces full. Sleeping...')
42.        os.sleep(300)  -- wait for five minutes
43.      end
44.    end
45. end
```

After you've entered these instructions, press CTRL, make sure [**Save**] is selected, and press ENTER. Then quit the editor by pressing CTRL, selecting [**Exit**], and pressing ENTER. In addition, you'll need the hare module, which you can download by running `pastebin get wwzvaKuW hare`.

RUNNING THE COBMINER PROGRAM

After you've set up the cobblestone generator with five furnaces, position the turtle facing the cobblestone block and run **cobminer**. The turtle will begin to mine the cobblestone until it has 64 blocks; then it will drop them into the furnaces. Until you write the brickcrafter program in Chapter 10, you'll have to manually load fuel into the furnaces and remove the smelted stone blocks from them. To create fuel for the furnaces, smelt the wood blocks from the tree-farming turtles in separate furnaces to produce charcoal for fueling the furnaces. Let's look at each part of the cobminer program.

If you get errors when running this program, carefully compare your code to the code in this book to find any typos. If you still cannot fix your program, delete the file by running `delete cobminer` and then download it by running `pastebin get YhvSiw7e cobminer`.

SETTING UP YOUR PROGRAM AND MAKING A CONSTANT VARIABLE

The first couple of lines of the program contain the usual comment that describes what the program is.

cobminer
```
1. --[[Stone Brick Factory program by Al Sweigart
2. Mines cobblestone from a generator, turtle 1 of 2]]
```

```
3.
4. os.loadAPI('hare')  -- load the hare module
5. local numToDrop
```

Line 4 loads the `hare` module so the program can call `hare.selectItem()`. Line 5 declares a variable called `numToDrop`, which is used later in the program.

Line 6 declares the `NUM_FURNACES` variable, which contains an integer that represents the number of furnaces that are placed behind the turtle.

cobminer

```
6. local NUM_FURNACES = 5
```

This program has five furnaces, but you can add more furnaces if you like. If you add more furnaces to your cobblestone generator, set the value of `NUM_FURNACES` to the new number of furnaces.

The `NUM_FURNACES` variable is uppercase because it's a *constant* variable, which means its value never changes while the program is running. Uppercase names for constants are just a convention. Constants are still regular variables. The capitalized name helps remind you that you shouldn't write code that changes the variable. It might seem odd to have a variable whose value never changes, but using constants will make your code easier to understand and will make future changes convenient.

For example, you need to indicate the number of furnaces in your code, but if you use the number instead of `NUM_FURNACES` throughout your code and then you later change the number of furnaces, you would have to update your code everywhere that number is used. When you use a constant like `NUM_FURNACES`, you can update your code by just changing the assignment statement, which in this case is on line 6. Constants make your code clear and easy to modify.

MINING THE COBBLESTONE FROM THE GENERATOR

Line 9 begins the program's main `while` loop, which contains the code to make the turtle mine cobblestone, move over the furnaces, and drop cobblestone into the furnaces.

cobminer

```
8. print('Starting mining program...')
9. while true do
10.    -- mine cobblestone
11.    if turtle.detect() then
12.      print('Cobblestone detected. Mining...')
13.      turtle.dig()  -- mine cobblestone
```

The first part, mining cobblestone, begins on line 11. The `turtle.detect()` function returns `true` if a cobblestone block is in front of the turtle. In that case, the program displays `Cobblestone detected. Mining...` and the call `turtle.dig()` on line 13 mines the cobblestone.

However, if there is no cobblestone because it was previously mined (and the new cobblestone block hasn't formed yet), turtle.detect() returns false. When the if statement's condition is false, the block of code after the else statement on line 14 runs.

cobminer

```
14.  else
15.    print('No cobblestone. Sleeping...')
16.    os.sleep(0.5)  -- half-second pause
17.  end
```

This code displays No cobblestone. Sleeping... and calls os.sleep(0.5) to pause the program for half a second so a new cobblestone block has enough time to form. This new cobblestone block will be mined when the program loops around again. When the turtle is done mining cobblestone, it needs to smelt the cobblestone in the furnaces.

INTERACTING WITH FURNACES

Furnaces have three slots: a *fuel slot* where burnable items like coal power the furnace, an *input slot* for items to be smelted, and an *output slot* where the smelted items remain until the player takes them. The turtle's position next to the furnace determines whether the turtle is putting an item into the furnace as fuel, putting an item in as a block to smelt, or removing the final product. If the turtle is on the side of the furnace, it can drop items into and take items from the furnace's fuel slot. If a turtle is above a furnace, it can drop items into and take items from the furnace's input slot. If a turtle is below a furnace, it can take smelted items from the furnace's output slot. Figure 9-4 shows these positions.

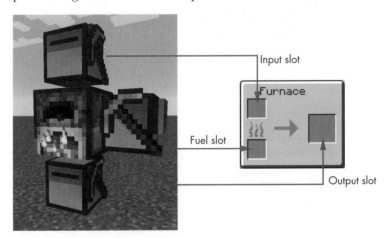

Figure 9-4: The turtle's position indicates which furnace slot it interacts with.

Next, the turtle will drop the cobblestone blocks into the furnaces.

MAKING CODE READABLE WITH CONSTANTS

After checking for a cobblestone block to mine, the program then checks whether the turtle has collected 64 cobblestone blocks, which is the maximum an inventory slot can hold. If so, the turtle is ready to drop them into the furnaces behind it after checking that it has enough fuel to travel across the furnaces and back to the cobblestone generator.

cobminer

```
19.   -- check for a full stack of cobblestone
20.   hare.selectItem('minecraft:cobblestone')
21.   if turtle.getItemCount() == 64 then
22.     -- check turtle's fuel
23.     if turtle.getFuelLevel() < (2 * NUM_FURNACES) then
24.       error('Turtle needs more fuel!')
25.     end
```

The hare.selectItem() function on line 20 finds the inventory slot with cobblestone and selects the slot. Line 21 calls turtle.getItemCount() to check the number of cobblestone blocks in this slot. If the total is 64 cobblestone blocks, the program calls turtle.getFuelLevel() to check the turtle's fuel level.

Line 23 checks whether the turtle's fuel level is less than 2 * NUM_FURNACES. The reason is that the turtle needs enough fuel to move over each furnace and then move back across each furnace to return to its starting position, as shown in Figure 9-5.

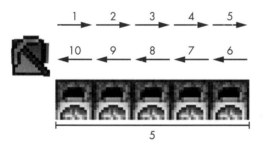

Figure 9-5: The amount of fuel needed to move over the furnaces and back is twice the number of furnaces.

If the turtle doesn't have enough fuel, line 24 calls error() and displays Turtle needs more fuel!. Then line 25 terminates the program.

DROPPING THE COBBLESTONE INTO THE FURNACES

When the turtle has 64 cobblestone blocks and enough fuel to travel across the furnaces and back, the turtle can move backward and drop off the cobblestone, like in Figure 9-6.

Figure 9-6: The turtle drops cobblestone blocks into the furnaces.

The for loop on line 29 is slightly different from for loops we've used before. A for loop can count up, as in for i = 1, 10 do, but it can also count in different increments when you include a third number, a step number, to the statement. Instead of adding 1 on each iteration, the for loop will add the number indicated in the step argument. If you use a negative number, as in for i = 10, 1, -1 do, you can make the loop count down.

<table>
<tr><td>cobminer</td><td>

```
27.     -- put cobblestone in furnaces
28.     print('Dropping off cobblestone...')
29.     for furnacesToFill = NUM_FURNACES, 1, -1 do
30.       turtle.back()  -- move over furnace
31.       numToDrop = math.floor(turtle.getItemCount() / furnacesToFill)
32.       turtle.dropDown(numToDrop)  -- put cobblestone in furnace
33.     end
```

</td></tr>
</table>

The for loop on line 29 tells the turtle to move backward NUM_FURNACES (or five) times. However, it begins counting at 5 down to 1 instead of 1 up to 5, so we can use the for loop variable, furnacesToFill, on line 31 to calculate how many cobblestone blocks to drop into each furnace. This calculation uses the math.floor() function. Let's look at how this function works.

ROUNDING NUMBERS WITH THE MATH.FLOOR() AND MATH.CEIL() FUNCTIONS

The math.floor() function rounds down the number it's passed and returns it, whereas the math.ceil() function ("ceil" as in "ceiling") rounds up the number it's passed and returns it. Enter the following into the Lua shell to see how these functions work.

```
lua> math.floor(4.2)
4
lua> math.floor(4.9)
4
lua> math.floor(10.5)
10
lua> math.floor(12.0)
12
lua> math.ceil(4.2)
5
lua> math.ceil(4.9)
5
lua> math.ceil(10.5)
11
❶ lua> math.ceil(12.0)
12
```

Passing a value to math.floor() results in the number without its decimal point, whereas passing a number to math.ceil() rounds up the number to the next number. When you pass math.ceil() a number with a decimal value of 0, it doesn't round up but instead rounds to the closest integer, as you can see at ❶. The functions' rounding helps us evenly distribute the turtle's cobblestone into the furnaces.

CALCULATING THE COBBLESTONE TO DISTRIBUTE IN EACH FURNACE

In Minecraft, each furnace's input slot can hold up to 64 items to smelt. For efficiency, we want all the furnaces smelting at the same time instead of just one. To calculate how many cobblestone blocks to drop into each furnace, we'll divide the number of cobblestone blocks in the current slot by NUM_FURNACES. Because this division operation might not result in a whole number, such as 64 / 5 = 12.8, we'll pass this number to math.floor(), which in this case rounds down the number to 12. Then we'll drop that number of cobblestone blocks into each furnace so all the furnaces can smelt at the same time.

But this calculation has a couple of problems. For example, if you have 64 cobblestone blocks and 5 furnaces, the turtle will drop 12 cobblestone blocks in each furnace and be left with 4 blocks. Turtles can mine cobblestone quicker than furnaces can smelt them, and each furnace can hold 64 items at most in its input slot. For each furnace that is full and can't accept any more cobblestone, the turtle will be left holding the portion of blocks for that furnace—in this case, 12. To address this issue, we'll make a different calculation. Let's look at lines 29 to 33 again:

cobminer
```
29.    for furnacesToFill = NUM_FURNACES, 1, -1 do
30.        turtle.back()  -- move over furnace
31.        numToDrop = math.floor(turtle.getItemCount() / furnacesToFill)
32.        turtle.dropDown(numToDrop)  -- put cobblestone in furnace
33.    end
```

Using numToDrop, line 31 calculates the number of cobblestone blocks to drop in each furnace with numToDrop = math.floor(turtle.getItemCount() / furnacesToFill). Instead of calculating the number of cobblestone blocks to drop once and storing that number in the numToDrop variable, the value of numToDrop is recalculated each time the turtle moves to a new furnace. Table 9-1 shows how numToDrop is calculated on each iteration of the for loop when all the furnaces are empty.

Table 9-1: numToDrop Values When All Furnaces Are Empty

Iteration	math.floor(turtle.getItemCount() / furnacesToFill)	numToDrop	Number of cobblestone dropped into furnace
First	math.floor(64 / 5)	12	12
Second	math.floor(52 / 4)	13	13
Third	math.floor(39 / 3)	13	13
Fourth	math.floor(26 / 2)	13	13
Fifth	math.floor(13 / 1)	13	13
			Total: 64

However, let's pretend the second furnace is full because the player dropped some of their own mined cobblestone into it. Now no cobblestone can be dropped into the second furnace. But because numToDrop is recalculated on each iteration of the for loop, the code automatically drops more cobblestone into the later furnaces. Table 9-2 shows how numToDrop is calculated on each iteration. Notice that on the second iteration, the number of cobblestone blocks dropped in the furnace is 0 because the second furnace is full.

Table 9-2: numToDrop Values When the Second Furnace Is Full

Iteration	math.floor(turtle.getItemCount() / furnacesToFill)	numToDrop	Number of cobblestone dropped into furnace
First	math.floor(64 / 5)	12	12
Second	math.floor(52 / 4)	13	0
Third	math.floor(52 / 3)	17	17
Fourth	math.floor(35 / 2)	17	17
Fifth	math.floor(18 / 1)	18	18
			Total: 64

Lines 29 to 33 show that a bit of clever code can make the furnaces work at maximum efficiency. When the for loop has finished, the turtle will be over the last furnace and will need to move back to the cobblestone block.

MOVING THE COBBLESTONE MINER BACK INTO POSITION

Lines 36 to 38 keep moving the turtle forward until it is in front of the cobblestone block.

cobminer

```
35.     -- move back to cobblestone generator
36.     for moves = 1, NUM_FURNACES do
37.        turtle.forward()
38.     end
```

At this point, the turtle checks the current slot. Remember, the turtle can mine cobblestone quicker than furnaces can smelt them. It won't be long before all of the furnaces are completely full but the turtle has 64 cobblestone blocks to drop in them. If any cobblestone is still in the turtle's inventory, then all the furnaces are full and the turtle is unable to put this cobblestone in them.

cobminer

```
40.     if turtle.getItemCount() > 0 then
41.        print('All furnaces full. Sleeping...')
42.        os.sleep(300)  -- wait for 5 minutes
43.     end
44.   end
45. end
```

The turtle.getItemCount() returns the number of items in the current slot. If this number is greater than 0 (meaning the turtle still has some cobblestone), line 42 pauses the program for 300 seconds, or five minutes, to give the furnaces more time to smelt the previous cobblestone.

Line 43 ends the if statement block on line 40, line 44 ends the if statement block on line 21, and line 45 ends the while loop on line 9. Finally, the execution loops back to line 9 and the turtle continues mining cobblestone and filling the furnaces until it runs out of fuel.

As with the tree-farming program in Chapter 8, you can scale your cobblestone production by building multiple cobblestone generators. You can also add more furnaces behind the turtle and change the NUM_FURNACES constant. (Five or six furnaces are plenty to smelt cobblestone. Otherwise, your turtle won't be able to mine fast enough to keep up with the furnaces!)

BONUS ACTIVITY: COBBLE TOGETHER MORE COBBLESTONE FURNACES

Try creating a cobblestone furnace with more than five furnaces. You'll need to adjust the NUM_FURNACES variable in the cobminer program so the turtle uses these extra furnaces.

WHAT YOU LEARNED

In this chapter, you learned how to build a cobblestone generator that mixes lava and water streams to produce an endless supply of cobblestone blocks for your turtle to mine, and you used the cobminer program to make the turtle mine these cobblestone blocks and drop them into furnaces behind the turtle. You also learned about constants, which are variables that don't change their values and which help make your code more readable. In addition, you learned about the step argument in for loops, which lets you create for loops that count down instead of up. Finally, you learned how the math.floor() and math.ceil() functions can round a number down and up, respectively.

In Chapter 10, we'll use the cobminer program to create a stone brick factory, which is a two-turtle operation. We'll write a program that will instruct another turtle to take smelted stone blocks out of the furnaces and craft them into stone brick using the brickcrafter program.

MAKING A STONE BRICK FACTORY

You should now have a turtle that mines cobblestone from an infinite cobblestone generator and drops the cobblestone into furnaces to smelt stone. You've automated the smelting process, but you still have to manually take the stone from the furnaces to use it. That's useful, but it's not exactly what we would call a stone brick factory. Now you need to program a second turtle to pull out the smelted stone and craft stone bricks. Once you have your turtle team running, like in Figure 10-1, you'll have all the stone bricks you need to build with.

Figure 10-1: The complete setup for an automated stone brick factory

DESIGNING A PROGRAM TO CRAFT STONE BRICKS

The first turtle, running the cobminer program, is positioned above the furnaces. The second turtle will move beneath the furnaces so it can pull items from each furnace's output slot. Remember that mining stone or cobblestone blocks produces cobblestone blocks. Putting these cobblestone blocks into a furnace will produce stone blocks, and stone blocks can be used to craft stone brick blocks.

As in the cobminer program, the second turtle's program first needs to check that the turtle has enough fuel to move across the furnaces and back to its original position. As the turtle moves to each furnace, it gathers stone blocks that have been smelted from the cobblestone. When it has gathered a full stack of 64 stone blocks, it crafts them into 64 stone bricks, which it places in a chest. If there isn't enough stone in the furnaces' output slots, the turtle waits two minutes for more cobblestone to be smelted. Then the turtle repeats the entire process.

CRAFTING A CRAFTY TURTLE

To make a turtle that can create stone bricks, you first need to make a turtle that can craft. Turtles can craft items with the turtle.craft() function. However, to enable this function, the turtle must equip a crafting table the same way it equips a diamond pickaxe. Choose a turtle other than the one running the cobminer program and place a crafting table in the turtle's currently selected slot. Then run the following code in the Lua shell:

```
lua> turtle.equipLeft()
```

This code will unequip any tool on the turtle's left side and equip the crafting table in the currently selected slot. Figure 10-2 shows the turtle and its inventory before and after running `turtle.equipLeft()`.

Figure 10-2: The turtle before (left) and after (right) calling `turtle.equipLeft()` to unequip the pickaxe and equip the crafting table

Now you can have your turtle call the `turtle.craft()` function. Your pickaxe-less turtle won't be able to call `turtle.dig()`, but this stone brick–making turtle doesn't need to mine anything.

NOTE   *If you want a turtle that can craft* and *dig, you can equip a turtle with two tools. You do this by calling both `turtle.equipLeft()` to equip one tool on the left side of the turtle and `turtle.equipRight()` to equip another tool on the right side. Figure 10-3 shows a turtle with a diamond pickaxe on the left side and a crafting table on the right, letting the turtle call both `turtle.dig()` and `turtle.craft()`.*

Figure 10-3: A turtle with a diamond pickaxe on its left side (left) and a crafting table on its right side (right)

With the crafting table equipped, the turtle can craft items in its inventory using the same recipe layouts as a crafting table. When the turtle calls turtle.craft(), the crafted item will be placed in the currently selected slot. For example, to craft stone bricks, lay out four stone blocks in a square in the turtle's inventory, as shown in Figure 10-4. Make sure all the other inventory slots are empty, and run turtle.select(16) and turtle.craft() from the Lua shell:

```
lua> turtle.select(16)
true
lua> turtle.craft()
true
```

Figure 10-4 shows the turtle's GUI before and after crafting stone bricks. Notice that inventory slot 16 is currently selected in the figure, and the crafted item is placed in the currently selected slot.

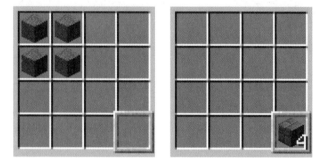

Figure 10-4: The turtle's inventory before (left) and after (right) calling the turtle.craft() function

If the items you lay out don't match any Minecraft recipe, turtle.craft() will return false and you'll see this error message:

```
lua> turtle.craft()
false
No matching recipes
```

Now that we've done all the setup and planning for the second turtle's program, let's write the code. We'll call the second turtle's program brickcrafter.

WRITING THE BRICKCRAFTER PROGRAM

From the command shell, run **edit brickcrafter** and enter the following code:

brickcrafter

```
1. --[[Stone Brick Factory program by Al Sweigart
2. Gets stone from furnace to craft stone bricks, turtle 2 of 2]]
3.
```

```
4. print('Starting stone brick crafting program...')
5.
6. local NUM_FURNACES = 5
7. local brickCount = 0
8. while true do
9.    -- check turtle's fuel
10.   if turtle.getFuelLevel() < (2 * NUM_FURNACES) then
11.     error('Turtle needs more fuel!')
12.   end
13.
14.   turtle.select(1)  -- put stone in slot 1
15.
16.   -- start collecting stone from furnaces
17.   for i = 1, NUM_FURNACES do
18.     turtle.suckUp(64 - turtle.getItemCount(1))  -- get stone from furnace
19.     if turtle.getItemCount(1) == 64 then
20.       break  -- stop once there are 64 stone blocks
21.     end
22.     if i ~= NUM_FURNACES then
23.       turtle.back()  -- move to next furnace
24.     end
25.   end
26.
27.   -- craft stone bricks
28.   if turtle.getItemCount(1) == 64 then
29.     turtle.transferTo(2, 16)  -- put in slot 2
30.     turtle.transferTo(5, 16)  -- put in slot 5
31.     turtle.transferTo(6, 16)  -- put in slot 6
32.     turtle.select(16)  -- stone bricks to go in slot 16
33.     turtle.craft()  -- craft stone bricks
34.     brickCount = brickCount + 64
35.     print('Total stone bricks: ' .. brickCount)
36.   else
37.     print('Not enough stone yet. Sleeping...')
38.     os.sleep(120)  -- wait for 2 minutes
39.   end
40.
41.   -- move back to chest (by first furnace)
42.   for i = 1, NUM_FURNACES - 1 do
43.     turtle.forward()
44.   end
45.   turtle.turnLeft()  -- face chest
46.   turtle.select(16)  -- select stone bricks
47.   turtle.drop()  -- put stone bricks into chest
48.   turtle.turnRight()  -- face generator again
49. end
```

After you've entered all of these instructions, press the CTRL button, make sure [Save] is selected, and press ENTER. Then quit the editor by pressing CTRL, selecting [Exit], and then pressing ENTER.

RUNNING THE BRICKCRAFTER PROGRAM

Before you can run the brickcrafter program, you'll need to have a turtle that is running the cobminer program with the cobblestone generator and furnace setup from Chapter 9. You'll also need a second chest (single- or double-size) and a second turtle to run the brickcrafter program. Place the new chest next to the cobblestone generator and position the new turtle under the first furnace, as shown in Figure 10-5. The chest will hold all of the crafted stone bricks. Make sure your turtle's inventory is completely empty, or the brickcrafter program won't run as expected.

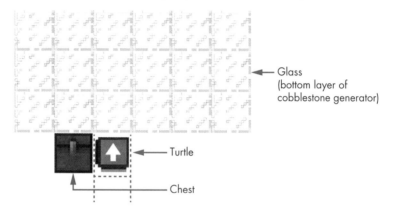

Glass
(bottom layer of
cobblestone generator)

Turtle

Chest

Figure 10-5: The position of the chest and turtle. The white arrow shows which direction the turtle should face. The dotted lines show where the furnaces are positioned on the second layer of the cobblestone generator.

The complete setup for your cobblestone generator and stone brick crafter will look like Figure 10-6.

Figure 10-6: Put a chest next to the cobblestone generator to provide storage for the stone bricks.

This brickcrafter program instructs the turtle to move underneath the furnaces and take out each furnace's smelted stone. Then the turtle lays out the stone blocks according to the stone brick recipe, calls turtle.craft() to create stone bricks, and places the stone bricks into the chest next to the generator. Because the turtle must move back and forth, it will check its fuel level and stop the program if it runs out of fuel.

If you get errors when running this program, carefully compare your code to the code in this book to find any typos. If you still cannot fix your program, delete the file by running delete brickcrafter and then download it by running pastebin get 1zS07K3U brickcrafter.

SETUP FOR THE BRICKCRAFTER PROGRAM

The first few lines of the program contain the usual descriptive comments and a print() call that displays a message telling the player the program has started. We also set up two variables we'll use later in the program.

brickcrafter
```
1. --[[Stone Brick Factory program by Al Sweigart
2. Gets stone from furnace to craft stone bricks, turtle 2 of 2]]
3.
4. print('Starting stone brick crafting program...')
5.
6. local NUM_FURNACES = 5
7. local brickCount = 0
```

The NUM_FURNACES constant serves the same purpose as the NUM_FURNACES constant in the cobminer program from Chapter 9. The brickCount variable keeps track of the number of stone bricks the turtle has crafted.

CHECKING THE TURTLE'S FUEL

Line 8 begins an infinite loop for the main part of the program. The program continues running until the turtle runs out of fuel or the player presses CTRL-T to terminate the program.

brickcrafter
```
 8. while true do
 9.    -- check turtle's fuel
10.    if turtle.getFuelLevel() < (2 * NUM_FURNACES) then
11.      error('Turtle needs more fuel!')
12.    end
```

Inside the loop, the program first checks that the turtle has enough fuel to reach each furnace and return to the chest. Lines 10 to 12 are similar to lines 23 to 25 in the cobminer program in Chapter 9. Line 10 checks that the turtle has at least twice as much fuel as the number of furnaces. If not, the call to error() on line 11 terminates the program.

COLLECTING STONE FROM THE FURNACES

If the turtle has enough fuel to move under all the furnaces and back, it selects inventory slot 1 so that when it takes the stone from a furnace, the stone ends up in this slot.

brickcrafter

```
14.   turtle.select(1)  -- put stone in slot 1
```

Next, the execution enters a for loop on line 17. On each iteration of the loop, the turtle pulls out smelted stone from the furnace above it to fill up inventory slot 1. When the turtle has filled its inventory slot to maximum capacity (64 blocks), it breaks out of the loop so it can then craft stone bricks from the stone. If inventory slot 1 is not yet full, the program execution continues to the next if statement and moves the turtle backward to the next furnace.

brickcrafter

```
16.   -- start collecting stone from furnaces
17.   for i = 1, NUM_FURNACES do
18.     turtle.suckUp(64 - turtle.getItemCount(1))  -- get stone from furnace
19.     if turtle.getItemCount(1) == 64 then
20.       break  -- stop once there are 64 stone blocks
21.     end
22.     if i ~= NUM_FURNACES then
23.       turtle.back()  -- move to next furnace
24.     end
25.   end
```

The turtle.suckUp() function takes all the blocks from a container above a turtle and stores them in the turtle's currently selected slot. You can pass this function a number to limit the amount of blocks sucked into the turtle's selected slot. You can also use the turtle.suck() and turtle.suckDown() functions to take blocks from containers in front of and below the turtle, respectively.

In this case, because the turtle is under the furnaces, it pulls out items from the furnace's output slot. The turtle can hold a maximum of 64 stone blocks in inventory slot 1, so we do some math to ensure that the turtle doesn't try to overfill its slot. The turtle.getItemCount(1) part of the command returns the number of blocks the turtle already has in its slot, which we subtract from 64 to get the number of blocks the turtle should retrieve from the furnace. For example, if inventory slot 1 already has 30 stone blocks in it and there are 64 stone blocks in the furnace, the turtle shouldn't take out all 64 stone blocks. Instead, it should take out no more than 64 – 30, or 34, stone blocks.

If the number of items in inventory slot 1 is 64, then we don't want to add more blocks to the slot. The if statement on line 19 evaluates to true, and the execution breaks out of this for loop.

If the inventory slot is not yet full, the turtle needs to move backward to go under the next furnace. The turtle should continue pulling items from the furnace it's beneath and then move to the next furnace until it's under the last furnace. The turtle is under the last furnace when i, the for loop's variable, is set to the same number as NUM_FURNACES. This is why the if statement on line 22 only runs line 23 if i doesn't equal NUM_FURNACES. When the turtle reaches the last furnace, it exits the for loop.

CRAFTING STONE BRICKS

When the turtle has 64 stone blocks, it needs to craft them into stone bricks. Remember that turtles craft stone bricks using the same recipe as you would use on a crafting table, but instead the turtle crafts stone bricks in its own inventory. To craft stone blocks into stone bricks, put equal amounts of stone blocks into four inventory slots to form a square. Figure 10-7 shows the recipe to craft stone bricks.

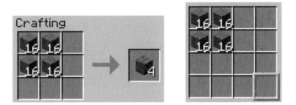

Figure 10-7: The recipe for crafting stone bricks (left) and the same recipe in the turtle's inventory (right)

When the stone blocks are in the correct recipe pattern, calling turtle .craft() will craft as many stone bricks as possible and store them in the current slot. If you want the turtle to craft only a certain number of items, even if it has enough material for more, pass a number argument to turtle.craft(). For example, turtle.craft(1) will use only one stone block from each slot and craft a single stone brick.

Line 28 checks if there are 64 stone blocks in inventory slot 1. If there are, the execution enters the code block starting on line 29.

brickcrafter
```
27.    -- craft stone bricks
28.    if turtle.getItemCount(1) == 64 then
29.      turtle.transferTo(2, 16)  -- put in slot 2
30.      turtle.transferTo(5, 16)  -- put in slot 5
31.      turtle.transferTo(6, 16)  -- put in slot 6
32.      turtle.select(16)  -- stone bricks to go in slot 16
33.      turtle.craft()  -- craft stone bricks
34.      brickCount = brickCount + 64
35.      print('Total stone bricks: ' .. brickCount)
```

The turtle.transferTo() function moves items from the current slot to another slot. You can specify which slot the items are moved to by passing an integer as the first parameter of the function, and you can specify the number of items that are moved to the slot with the second parameter. The turtle.transferTo(2, 16) function call on line 29 moves 16 stone blocks from the current slot (which is 1, as set on line 14) to slot 2.

Lines 30 and 31 move 16 stone blocks to slots 5 and 6, which results in the turtle's inventory looking like the recipe in Figure 10-7. Then, line 32 calls turtle.select(16) to change the current slot to slot 16 so when turtle.craft() is called on line 33, the crafted stone bricks will be placed in slot 16. Lines 34 and 35 calculate and print the number of stone bricks crafted by the turtle so far.

If the turtle didn't have 64 stone blocks in inventory slot 1 after pulling them from the furnaces, line 38 pauses for 120 seconds (two minutes) to give the furnaces more time to smelt stone blocks.

brickcrafter

```
36.   else
37.      print('Not enough stone yet. Sleeping...')
38.      os.sleep(120)  -- wait for 2 minutes
39.   end
```

In this case, the program would continue and the turtle would move back to the first furnace. Whether or not stone bricks have been crafted, the turtle needs to move back to the first furnace next to the cobblestone generator so it can collect more smelted stone.

MOVING THE TURTLE BACK INTO POSITION

To move the turtle back to its original position, we need to move the turtle forward until it arrives at the first furnace again, which we do on line 42 with a for loop. Once there, the turtle stores its stone bricks in the chest.

brickcrafter

```
41.   -- move back to chest (by first furnace)
42.   for i = 1, NUM_FURNACES - 1 do
43.      turtle.forward()
44.   end
45.   turtle.turnLeft()  -- face chest
46.   turtle.select(16)  -- select stone bricks
47.   turtle.drop()  -- put stone bricks into chest
48.   turtle.turnRight()  -- face generator again
49. end
```

Lines 42 to 44 move the turtle forward so that it's back in its original position. That is, the turtle moves NUM_FURNACES - 1 so that it's below the first furnace. On line 6, we set NUM_FURNACES to 5, so the turtle moves four spaces here. Line 45 turns the turtle to face the chest and line 46 selects all the stone bricks it crafted, which are in inventory slot 16. Then line 47 puts the selected stone bricks into the chest (or does nothing, if no bricks were crafted), and line 48 turns the turtle right to face the cobblestone generator again.

The end statement on line 49 corresponds with the infinite while loop that began on line 8, so when the execution reaches this point, it jumps back to line 8 to begin the entire process of collecting stone, crafting it into stone bricks, and dropping the stone bricks into the chest all over again.

Cakes are one of the most complex recipes in Minecraft, requiring milk, eggs, sugar, and wheat, as shown in Figure 10-8.

Figure 10-8: The Minecraft recipe for cake

Create a program that instructs a turtle to make a cake. Store the ingredients in separate chests and then program the turtle to move to each chest, obtain the cake ingredients, craft the cake, and place the finished cake into another chest. If a chest doesn't contain an ingredient, make the turtle wait a few minutes before checking again to see if the player has put more ingredients in.

CREATING A FACTORY BUILDING

The cobblestone generator and turtles are the main part of your factory line, but they're currently outside, where they're exposed to the rain and creepers. You're still missing your factory building! Now that you have an unlimited source of cobblestone and crafted stone bricks, you can create a building to house your cobblestone generators, as shown in Figures 10-9 and 10-10.

Figure 10-9: A building to house the cobblestone generator and turtles, made from the products of the cobblestone generator

Figure 10-10: The interior, with two cobblestone generators and a decorative lava waterfall

Fairly soon, your turtles will have produced plenty of stone bricks with which to build, as shown in Figure 10-11.

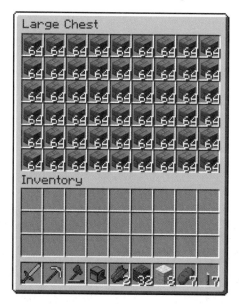

Figure 10-11: Your stone brick supply problems are over, thanks to the power of programming!

Creating a building for your cobblestone generator is optional, but at least you won't have to mine the blocks for it yourself if you do decide to build it. And in Chapters 11 and 12, you'll learn how to program the turtles to build walls and rooms for you!

WHAT YOU LEARNED

In this chapter, you learned how to swap out tools and equip a crafting table using the turtle.equipLeft() and turtle.equipRight() functions. Equipping a crafting table makes the turtle.craft() function available to the turtle.

To take items out of containers like chests or furnaces, you use the turtle.suck() function. You can pass a number argument to this function to control the number of items that are taken, and you can call turtle.suckUp() or turtle.suckDown() to interact with containers above or below the turtle.

Before calling turtle.craft(), you need to arrange items in the turtle's inventory according to recipes, just as the items would be arranged on a crafting table. You can use turtle.transferTo() to move items to different inventory slots to accomplish this. After calling turtle.craft(), the crafted items will appear in the currently selected slot.

With all the stone bricks we have now, let's start programming turtles to construct giant buildings for us in Chapter 11!

CONSTRUCTING WALLS

Placing blocks can be time consuming and dangerous, especially if you fall from a great height when you're creating large buildings in survival mode. Instead of building walls yourself, you can program a turtle to take on these hazardous and dull building jobs. In this chapter, you'll design an algorithm to create walls of any size by adding more functions to the hare module. Although we'll focus on creating stone brick walls in this chapter, the functions will work with any type of block, including dirt, glass, or even watermelons, as you can see in Figure 11-1.

Figure 11-1: Turtles building walls of dirt, stone bricks, glass, and watermelons

Let's begin by adding two functions to the hare module: one that counts the number of blocks in a turtle's inventory and one that builds walls.

EXTENDING THE HARE MODULE

We'll start by creating three new functions that will count the items in the inventory, select and place items, and create walls. We'll use these functions in other programs in this book, so we'll put them into the hare module that we started in Chapter 7. The first 35 lines of hare will remain unchanged. Therefore, I'll only show the code for lines 36 through 107.

From the command shell, run **edit hare**. Move the cursor to the bottom of the file and continue the code by entering the following:

hare

```
...snip...
36.
37.
38. -- countInventory() returns the total
39. -- number of items in the inventory
40. function countInventory()
41.   local total = 0
42.
43.   for slot = 1, 16 do
44.     total = total + turtle.getItemCount(slot)
45.   end
46.   return total
47. end
```

```
48.
49.
50. -- selectAndPlaceDown() selects a nonempty slot
51. -- and places a block from it under the turtle
52. function selectAndPlaceDown()
53.
54.   for slot = 1, 16 do
55.     if turtle.getItemCount(slot) > 0 then
56.       turtle.select(slot)
57.       turtle.placeDown()
58.       return
59.     end
60.   end
61. end
62.
63.
64. -- buildWall() creates a wall stretching
65. -- in front of the turtle
66. function buildWall(length, height)
67.   if hare.countInventory() < length * height then
68.     return false  -- not enough blocks
69.   end
70.
71.   turtle.up()
72.
73.   local movingForward = true
74.
75.   for currentHeight = 1, height do
76.     for currentLength = 1, length do
77.       selectAndPlaceDown()  -- place the block
78.       if movingForward and currentLength ~= length then
79.         turtle.forward()
80.       elseif not movingForward and currentLength ~= length then
81.         turtle.back()
82.       end
83.     end
84.     if currentHeight ~= height then
85.       turtle.up()
86.     end
87.     movingForward = not movingForward
88.   end
89.
90.   -- done building wall; move to end position
91.   if movingForward then
92.     -- turtle is near the start position
93.     for currentLength = 1, length do
94.       turtle.forward()
95.     end
96.   else
97.     -- turtle is near the end position
98.     turtle.forward()
99.   end
100.
```

```
101.    -- move down to the ground
102.    for currentHeight = 1, height do
103.      turtle.down()
104.    end
105.
106.    return true
107. end
```

After you've entered all of these instructions, save the program and exit the editor. You can also download this module by running pastebin get wwzvaKuW hare.

COUNTING INVENTORY ITEMS WITH COUNTINVENTORY()

Before the turtle begins building, we need the turtle to check whether it has enough blocks in its inventory. Assuming that every item in the turtle's inventory is a block that will be used in the wall, countInventory() returns the total number of items in all the turtle's inventory slots.

hare
```
38. -- countInventory() returns the total
39. -- number of items in the inventory
40. function countInventory()
41.   local total = 0
```

We'll store the total count of the blocks in the total variable, which we initially set to 0. Then we'll declare a slot variable that will keep track of which slot is being checked in the inventory.

Next, a for loop on line 43 iterates over all 16 inventory slots using the slot variable.

hare
```
43.   for slot = 1, 16 do
44.     total = total + turtle.getItemCount(slot)
45.   end
46.   return total
47. end
```

For each slot, the program calls the turtle.getItemCount() function and passes it the slot variable. The count of the blocks in each inventory slot is added to total. After the loop ends on line 46, the function returns total, which now contains a count of all the blocks in the turtle's inventory. Note that the turtle.getItemCount() function counts all items, even if they're not stone blocks.

SELECTING AND PLACING A BLOCK

To begin building, we need the turtle to place blocks from a nonempty slot. To accomplish this, we'll add a function named selectAndPlaceDown()

to the hare module. This function selects the first available nonempty slot and then places a block from that slot below the turtle.

hare

```
50. -- selectAndPlaceDown() selects a nonempty slot
51. -- and places a block from it under the turtle
52. function selectAndPlaceDown()
53.
54.   for slot = 1, 16 do
55.     if turtle.getItemCount(slot) > 0 then
56.       turtle.select(slot)
57.       turtle.placeDown()
58.       return
59.     end
60.   end
61. end
```

Line 54 is a for loop that sets the slot variable to 1 on the first iteration, 2 on the second iteration, and so on up to 16. This is how the function selectAndPlaceDown() will scan all the slots of the turtle's inventory.

Inside this loop, line 55 checks how many items are in the slot by calling turtle.getItemCount(slot). If more than zero blocks are in the slot, turtle.select(slot) on line 56 selects that slot and turtle.placeDown() on line 57 places the block below the turtle. Once the block has been placed and the function's job is done, line 58 returns out of the function selectAndPlaceDown().

This selectAndPlaceDown() function works no matter what kind of building blocks are in the turtle's inventory or which slots they're in. When the turtle has nothing in its inventory, the loop ends and the function does nothing. The buildWall() and buildRoom() functions will call selectAndPlaceDown() as part of their code.

DESIGNING A WALL-BUILDING ALGORITHM

Next, we need to create the buildWall() function, which takes two parameters to control the size of the wall: one for the length and one for the height. Before writing the function, let's design the algorithm the turtle will follow to build a wall.

When a turtle builds a wall, it needs to start on the ground, move up, and then place a block underneath itself. Then it needs to move forward and continue placing blocks until it has a line of blocks equal to length. Once the turtle has a line of blocks, it repeats the process in the opposite direction. The turtle continues moving back and forth, placing lines of blocks until it reaches the specified height. For example, let's say that length is 4 and height is 2. Figure 11-2 shows a side view of where the turtle starts and what the 4 × 2 wall will look like when it's built.

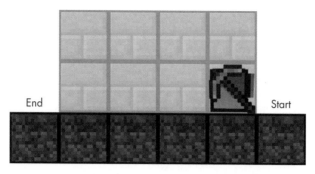

Figure 11-2: A side view of the turtle and the future 4 × 2 wall

The turtle needs to first move up and place a block below itself, as shown in Figure 11-3.

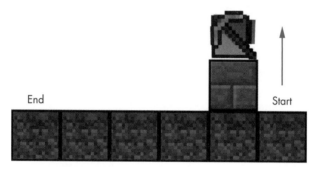

Figure 11-3: The turtle moves up and places a block below itself.

Because the turtle is building a wall four blocks long, the turtle moves forward three spaces, placing a block under itself after each move. If the turtle was building a wall that was six blocks long, it would move forward five spaces. Notice the pattern: the number of spaces the turtle moves forward is length - 1. To make the turtle place length blocks, we must make it move forward for each block except the last one, resulting in length - 1 forward moves. The buildWall() function can make walls of any length this way.

When the turtle has placed the first line of blocks for our 4 × 2 wall, the result will look like Figure 11-4.

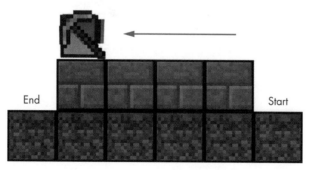

Figure 11-4: The turtle moves forward, placing blocks below itself.

The turtle repeats this process, except this time it moves backward, as shown in Figure 11-5.

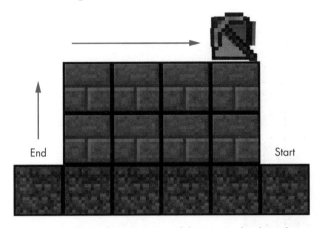

Figure 11-5: The turtle moves up and then moves backward as it places blocks beneath itself.

If the turtle had more rows to build, it would repeat the process, but by moving forward instead of backward. But because the turtle completed the number of rows needed for this example, the turtle is done building. In Chapter 12, we'll want the turtle to make four walls to build a room, so the algorithm should always have the turtle finish on the ground at the opposite end of the wall from where it started. That way, the turtle will be in position to build the next wall.

To have the turtle move to the opposite end of the wall from where it started, there are two potential paths the turtle might need to travel based on which direction it was last moving. If the turtle was last moving forward, it would move forward once and then move down height number of times. If the turtle was last moving backward, it needs to move forward length number of times and then move down height number of times. Either path will always make the turtle finish at the far end of the wall, as shown in Figure 11-6.

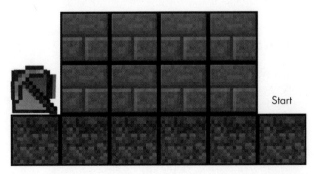

Figure 11-6: The turtle ends up on the ground at the far end of the wall.

The buildWall() function can construct walls of any length and height. For example, as long as you have enough blocks, you could make a tall wall like the one shown in Figure 11-7. It's all the same to the turtle.

Figure 11-7: A tall 4 × 12 wall is built using the same algorithm as the 4 × 2 wall.

Let's examine the function that performs this algorithm.

WRITING THE BUILDWALL() FUNCTION

The buildWall() function starts by counting the number of items in the turtle's inventory. It assumes these items are all blocks that will be used to build the wall. The number of blocks needed to build a wall length blocks long and height blocks tall is length * height, which is what we check for on line 67.

hare

```
64. -- buildWall() creates a wall stretching
65. -- in front of the turtle
66. function buildWall(length, height)
67.   if hare.countInventory() < length * height then
68.     return false  -- not enough blocks
69.   end
```

If the turtle doesn't have enough blocks to build the wall, the function returns false on line 68, which ends the function.

If the turtle does have enough blocks, the code on line 71 executes and the turtle moves up one block to start a new row. Then the program continues and sets the movingForward variable to true.

```
71.  turtle.up()
72.
73.  local movingForward = true
```

The movingForward variable keeps track of which direction the turtle should go. For the first row, the turtle will move forward, so the movingForward variable should be true. But for the next row, the turtle needs to move backward, so we'll need to change the variable to false later in the program. The variable's value will alternate at each row as the turtle alternates the direction it moves.

To keep track of how high the turtle has built the wall, the program needs another variable, which we'll call currentHeight. Line 75 starts a for loop in which currentHeight iterates from 1 to height. On the first iteration currentHeight is set to 1, on the next iteration it is set to 2, and so on, until the last iteration, where currentHeight is equal to height.

```
75.  for currentHeight = 1, height do
76.    for currentLength = 1, length do
77.      selectAndPlaceDown()  -- place the block
78.      if movingForward and currentLength ~= length then
79.        turtle.forward()
80.      elseif not movingForward and currentLength ~= length then
81.        turtle.back()
82.      end
83.    end
```

As the turtle is building up, we also need to keep track of the length of wall it is building for each height level. To do that, we will use another variable called currentLength, which is created in a second for loop on line 76. This second for loop is nested in the loop on line 75. On each iteration of the first for loop, the program runs the nested for loop. This inner nested for loop iterates currentLength from 1 to length. Figure 11-8 shows what values currentHeight and currentLength are set to at each point of building a 4 × 4 wall. The red arrow shows the path the turtle takes.

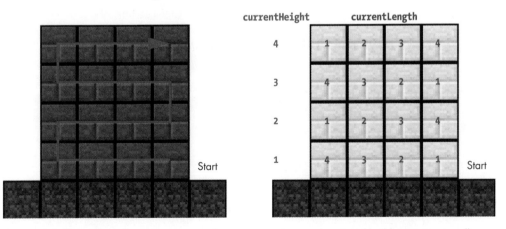

Figure 11-8: The values of currentHeight and currentLength at each point of building a 4 × 4 wall

Inside the loop, line 77 calls selectAndPlaceDown() to place a block below the turtle. The code on lines 78 to 82 moves the turtle either forward or backward depending on the value in movingForward and whether the turtle is at the edge of the wall. The currentLength variable counts how many blocks across the wall the turtle has already traveled. When it is equal to the length of the wall, the turtle needs to stop so it doesn't go past the edge.

Remember that the turtle doesn't need to move on the last iteration. Because the for loop on line 76 iterates from 1 up to length, currentLength is equal to length on the last iteration. This is why the conditions on lines 78 and 80 run only if currentLength doesn't equal (~=) length.

The end statement on line 82 ends the code block for the for loop on line 76. After this for loop, the turtle has placed blocks for the entire row. Now the turtle has to move up one space unless it is at the last iteration of the for loop on line 75. The turtle.up() call on line 85 runs only if currentHeight doesn't equal height (that is, if the for loop isn't at the last iteration).

hare

```
84.      if currentHeight ~= height then
85.         turtle.up()
86.      end
87.      movingForward = not movingForward
88.   end
```

Line 87 *toggles*, or sets to the opposite value, the Boolean value in movingForward. If movingForward is true, the line sets movingForward to false, and if movingForward is false, the line sets movingForward to true. If the turtle was moving forward to build the highest row of blocks, the toggle will set movingForward to false. If the turtle was moving backward to build the highest row of blocks, the toggle on line 87 will set movingForward to true. Line 87 sets movingForward to its opposite Boolean value by simply setting it to not movingForward.

The end statement on line 88 ends the for loop that started on line 75. Once the execution gets past this loop, the entire wall has been built. Now the turtle needs to move back to the ground next to the wall. First, it needs to move off the wall and then travel down to the ground.

Recall that line 87 toggled the value in movingForward to make the turtle change directions. So if movingForward is now set to true, the turtle is closest to the starting point and needs to move length blocks forward to get off the wall, which it does on lines 93 and 94.

hare

```
90.   -- done building wall, move to end position
91.   if movingForward then
92.      -- turtle is near the start position
93.      for currentLength = 1, length do
94.         turtle.forward()
95.      end
```

But if movingForward is now set to false, the turtle is already at the opposite end of the wall and only needs to move one space forward, which it does on line 98.

```
96.    else
97.       -- turtle is near the end position
98.       turtle.forward()
99.    end
```

Whether the turtle was moving forward or backward last, it will always need to move height blocks down to reach the ground level it started from, so the for loop on line 102 calls turtle.down() a number of times equal to height.

```
101.    -- move down to the ground
102.    for currentHeight = 1, height do
103.       turtle.down()
104.    end
105.
106.    return true
107. end
```

At this point, the wall has been built and the turtle is in the final position. Therefore, the buildWall() function returns true on line 106 to indicate the wall has been successfully built. The end statement on line 107 ends the buildWall() function's code block.

The buildWall() function we put into the hare module is useful because building walls is a task that you might want to do in many programs. But if you just want to build a wall from the command shell instead of starting the Lua shell and typing os.loadAPI('hare') and hare.buildWall(4, 2), it would be easier to create and run a program to call this function for you. Let's create the buildwall program to do this.

WRITING AND RUNNING THE BUILDWALL PROGRAM

From the command shell, run **edit buildwall** and enter the following code:

```
1. --[[Wall Building program by Al Sweigart
2. Builds a wall.]]
3.
4. os.loadAPI('hare')
5.
6. -- handle command line arguments
7. local cliArgs = {...}
8. local length = tonumber(cliArgs[1])
9. local height = tonumber(cliArgs[2])
10.
11. if length == nil or height == nil or cliArgs[1] == '?' then
12.    print('Usage: buildwall <length> <height>')
13.    return
14. end
15.
16. print('Building...')
```

```
17. if hare.buildWall(length, height) == false then
18.    error('Not enough blocks.')
19. end
20. print('Done.')
```

After you've entered all of these instructions, save the program and exit the editor.

After placing the turtle and putting stone brick blocks (or any other kind of building block) into its inventory, right-click the turtle to open its GUI. From the command shell, enter **buildwall 4 2** and press ENTER to watch the turtle build a wall four blocks long and two blocks high.

If you get errors when running this program, carefully compare your code to the code in this book to find any typos. If you still cannot fix your program, delete the file by running delete buildwall and then download it by running pastebin get 1aZ8BhNX buildwall.

LOADING THE HARE MODULE

The first part of the buildwall program loads the hare module and calls hare.buildWall() for you.

buildwall

```
1. --[[Wall Building program by Al Sweigart
2. Builds a wall.]]
3.
4. os.loadAPI('hare')
```

Although most of the work is done by the code in the hare module, the buildwall program has some additional features. When calling hare.buildWall(), the program needs to know what values to pass for the length and height parameters. The buildwall program can get these values from the command line arguments that the player enters when running the buildwall program from the command shell. Earlier, you passed the buildwall program the command line arguments 4 and 2. You've already used command line arguments when running other programs, such as in Chapter 2 when you passed the label program the command line arguments set Sofonisba in label set Sofonisba. Command line arguments are stored as a type of table value called an *array* in a Lua object named {...}, which is made up of two braces with three periods in between. Before looking at the code that takes the command line arguments, let's look at how arrays work.

USING THE ARRAY DATA TYPE

The table values that you first learned about in Chapter 7 can store multiple values. Arrays are another data type whose values can store multiple values. The values in a table are stored with key-value pairs, whereas the values in arrays are stored in number order. To access a value in an array, you would use its numerical position, which is called an *index*.

Technically, arrays in Lua are just another type of table. The tables with key-value pairs we've used in previous chapters are called map-like tables, *whereas arrays are called* array-like tables.

The code for arrays is similar to the code for tables. To create an array, use braces, {}, just as you would for tables, but omit the keys. You don't need to enter keys because the position of the values tells Lua what the value's index is. Enter the following into the interactive shell to create your own array:

```
lua> pets = {'mouse', 'cat', 'dog'}
```

To access the values in an array, enter the name of the array, and then put the value's numeric index in between square brackets, []:

```
lua> pets[1]
mouse
lua> pets[2]
cat
lua> 'I have a pet ' .. pets[3]
I have a pet dog
```

Array numbering starts at 1 in the Lua programming language, so to access the first value in the pets array, you would enter pets[1].

READING COMMAND LINE ARGUMENTS

Returning to the buildwall program, line 7 stores the command line argument's array-like table value in a variable named cliArgs. This variable lets your code access the individual values inside the table value using square brackets: cliArgs[1] is the first command line argument, cliArgs[2] is the second, and so on.

buildwall

```
6. -- handle command line arguments
7. local cliArgs = {...}
8. local length = tonumber(cliArgs[1])
9. local height = tonumber(cliArgs[2])
```

All command line argument values are stored as strings, even if they seem like numbers, such as '4' or '2'. To convert values from strings to number values, lines 8 and 9 pass the command line arguments to the tonumber() function, which returns number values of the strings passed to it. We'll store these number values in the length and height variables.

CREATING USAGE MESSAGES

If the player doesn't enter any command line arguments (or enters only one command line argument instead of two), the program won't have enough information to run. Maybe the player doesn't know they were supposed to pass numbers for the length and height, or maybe they forgot to type them. In those cases, it's helpful for programs to display a *usage message*, which reminds the player how to run the program. The usage message also appears if the player uses ? as the first command line argument.

buildwall

```
11. if length == nil or height == nil or cliArgs[1] == '?' then
12.    print('Usage: buildwall <length> <height>')
13.    return
14. end
```

If there are no command line arguments or the arguments are not numbers, cliArgs[1] and cliArgs[2] will be set to the nil value. Passing nil or a string that doesn't contain a number to the tonumber() function will result in it returning nil. For example, if the player doesn't enter any command line arguments, length will be set to nil on line 8. If the player passes only one argument, height will be set to nil on line 9. The condition on line 11 checks if length or height are nil or if the first command line argument is the '?' string.

In situations where the player doesn't enter valid command line arguments, the print() call displays a usage message that tells the player to type buildwall followed by the command line arguments for the length and height. The angle brackets, <>, around length and height indicate that the player shouldn't type the words "length" and "height" but should instead type numbers for the length and height command line arguments.

CALLING HARE.BUILDWALL() TO BUILD A WALL

All of the hard work for the buildwall program is in the hare module's buildWall(), selectAndPlaceDown(), and countInventory() functions. So the buildwall program's code is simple. After preparing the command line arguments, it just calls the hare.buildWall() function on line 16 and passes in the values for length and height.

buildwall

```
16. print('Building...')
17. if hare.buildWall(length, height) == false then
18.    error('Not enough blocks.')
19. end
20. print('Done.')
```

Line 16 calls print() so the user can see that the program has started. When the hare.buildWall() function returns false, there are not enough blocks and the program won't run. We check for this on line 17 and show the user an error when that is the case. Then, line 20 prints a message to tell the user the program has finished, whether it has built the wall or given the user an error message.

That's the entire buildwall program! The code in the hare module handles the rest of the instructions.

WHAT YOU LEARNED

In this chapter, you expanded your hare module with new functions. The countInventory() function gives you the total number of items in the turtle's inventory. This is a useful way to check whether the turtle has enough blocks to build with. The selectAndPlaceDown() function makes the turtle select a particular block in its inventory and place it in the Minecraft world. With these functions, you can write code to construct walls of any size!

You also learned how to write programs that can read command line arguments. You've been using command line arguments since Chapter 2 (such as when you used set Sofonisba in label set Sofonisba). But in this chapter, you learned that you can access the table value of the {...} object to get the command line arguments the player enters when they run the program.

When other people run your programs, they probably won't know how to read Lua code to figure out what command line arguments are required for your program. Therefore, programs can display a usage message that gives a brief description of the command line arguments.

In Chapter 12, you'll build on the wall-building program (I never apologize for my puns) to create rooms with four walls.

12

CONSTRUCTING ROOMS

When you put together four walls, you have a room! In this chapter, you'll create the buildRoom() function, which calls buildWall() four times to construct a room like the one shown in Figure 12-1. This chapter is short and sweet because you did most of the coding work when you wrote the buildWall() function in Chapter 11. When you're done creating the buildRoom() function, you'll be able to use it to build complex structures, such as a castle!

Figure 12-1: A 5 × 6 × 4 room built of stone bricks

DESIGNING A ROOM-BUILDING ALGORITHM

Let's design an algorithm that takes length, width, and height values to create rooms of any size. We'll put the code for this algorithm inside a function named buildRoom() in the hare module. For example, if the turtle needs to build a room that is three blocks long and four blocks wide, it could build four walls like those shown in Figure 12-2. The turtle starts from the bottom-left corner of the room and then builds walls clockwise.

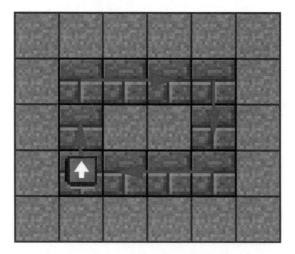

Figure 12-2: A top-down view of a turtle building a 3 × 4 room. The turtle is facing the same direction as the white arrow when it starts building.

Because walls overlap at the corners of a room, the length and width of a room are different from the dimensions of its walls. For example, to build a 3 × 4 room like the one in Figure 12-2, you can't just build two walls of length three and two walls of length four because the corners would overlap. To properly size the wall lengths of a room, you must account for the corners. Look at the size of each wall in Figure 12-3, which shows a 3 × 4 room and a 4 × 6 room.

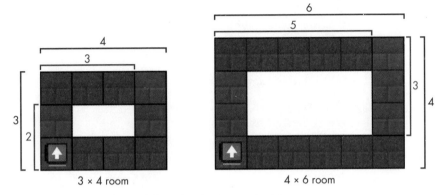

Figure 12-3: A 3 × 4 room (left) and a 4 × 6 room (right)

As you can see, the room that is 3 × 4 in size is made up of two walls that are two blocks long and two walls that are three blocks long. The room that is 4 × 6 in size is made up of two walls that are three blocks long and two walls that are five blocks long.

Notice the pattern of our algorithm. The four walls are of two different sizes: one size is the width of the room minus one, and the other size is the length of the room minus one. The algorithm will call the buildWall() function that we created in Chapter 11. The turtle begins in the lower-left corner, as shown in Figure 12-3, and builds the wall on the left side of the room (shown in red). Then, the algorithm tells the turtle to turn right and build the wall at the top of the room (shown in blue). The turtle turns right again, builds the red wall on the right side of the room, turns right, and builds the blue wall at the bottom of the room. When the turtle is done making all four walls, it ends up back where it started. By using this pattern in its algorithm, the buildRoom() function can make rooms of any size.

EXTENDING THE HARE MODULE

We'll put the buildRoom() function in the hare module, just as we did with the buildWall() function, so other programs can use it. From the command shell, run **edit hare**. Move the cursor to the bottom of the file and continue the code by entering the following:

hare

```
...snip...
110. -- buildRoom() constructs four walls
111. -- and a ceiling
```

```
112. function buildRoom(length, width, height)
113.    if hare.countInventory() < (((length - 1) * height * 2) +
           ((width - 1) * height * 2)) then
114.      return false  -- not enough blocks
115.    end
116.
117.    -- build the four walls
118.    buildWall(length - 1, height)
119.    turtle.turnRight()
120.
121.    buildWall(width - 1, height)
122.    turtle.turnRight()
123.
124.    buildWall(length - 1, height)
125.    turtle.turnRight()
126.
127.    buildWall(width - 1, height)
128.    turtle.turnRight()
129.
130.    return true
131. end
```

After you've entered all of these instructions, save the program and exit the editor. You can also download this module by running pastebin get wwzvaKuW hare.

CALCULATING THE TOTAL NUMBER OF BLOCKS NEEDED TO BUILD A ROOM

Before the buildRoom() function can create a room, the turtle must first check that it has enough building blocks in its inventory. We'll need to calculate the number of blocks needed for all four walls of the room. We calculated the number of blocks needed for a single wall on line 67 of hare as:

```
length * height
```

But this time the length of the wall is one block shorter than the length of the room. The first of the four walls should be length - 1 blocks long, so our calculation needs to be:

```
(length - 1) * height
```

And because the turtle will build two of these walls, we multiply this number by 2:

```
(length - 1) * height * 2
```

The other two walls will be one block shorter than the width of the room, which is width - 1 blocks in length, so we add the blocks for those walls to the calculation, as follows.

$$((length - 1) * height * 2) + ((width - 1) * height * 2)$$

This is the final formula for the number of blocks a room will require, which we'll use in the buildRoom() function.

WRITING THE BUILDROOM() FUNCTION

Line 113 calls hare.countInventory() to find out how many blocks are in the turtle's inventory. If this number is less than the number of blocks needed for the room, which we calculated the formula for in the preceding section, the execution moves to line 114, which returns false from buildRoom(). The code that called buildRoom() can use this return value to learn that the room was not built.

hare
```
110. -- buildRoom() constructs four walls
111. -- and a ceiling
112. function buildRoom(length, width, height)
113.   if hare.countInventory() < (((length - 1) * height * 2) +
          ((width - 1) * height * 2)) then
114.     return false  -- not enough blocks
115.   end
```

Otherwise, the execution continues past this code block. Because there are enough blocks to build the room, the turtle calls buildWall(). Line 118 builds the first wall of the room.

hare
```
118.   buildWall(length - 1, height)
```

After building the wall from the bottom up, the buildWall() function moves the turtle back down to the ground. If the turtle is building a 3 × 4 room, after running line 118, the room will look like the top-down view in Figure 12-4.

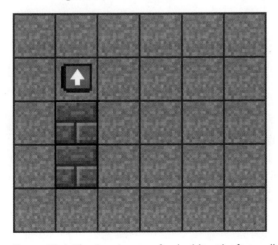

Figure 12-4: The 3 × 4 room after building the first wall

Before the turtle can build the second wall, it must turn right. The call to turtle.turnRight() on line 119 makes the turtle face the correct direction so it can build the next wall on line 121.

hare
```
119.    turtle.turnRight()
120.
121.    buildWall(width - 1, height)
```

Note that this wall's length is width - 1, where width is the width of the room. If the turtle is building a 3 × 4 room, the room will look like Figure 12-5 after line 121 executes.

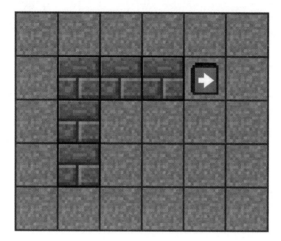

Figure 12-5: The 3 × 4 room after building the second wall

Similarly, lines 124 to 128 build the other two walls:

hare
```
122.    turtle.turnRight()
123.
124.    buildWall(length - 1, height)
125.    turtle.turnRight()
126.
127.    buildWall(width - 1, height)
128.    turtle.turnRight()
129.
130.    return true
131. end
```

After this code executes, the room is complete and the buildRoom() function returns true on line 130 to tell the code that called buildRoom() that the room was successfully built. The turtle will be back at its starting location and facing its original direction, but it will be on top of the first wall it built, as shown in Figure 12-6.

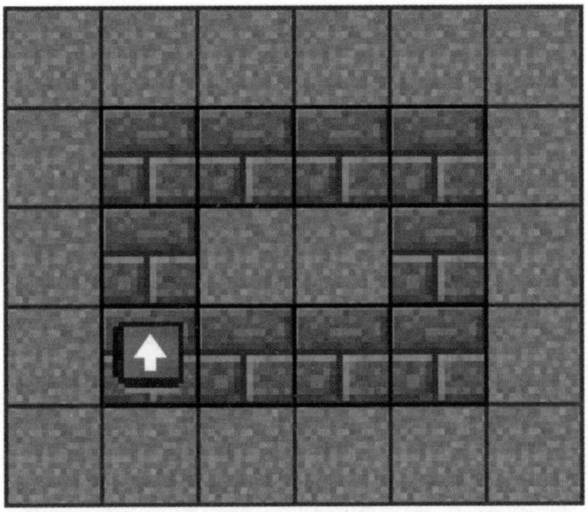

Figure 12-6: With the 3 × 4 room completed, the turtle returns to its starting point.

The end statement on line 131 ends the buildRoom() function's code block.

WRITING THE BUILDROOM PROGRAM

In Chapter 11, you made a buildwall program that calls hare.buildWall() so the player can easily build a wall from the command shell. We'll make a similar buildroom program to call hare.buildRoom(). From the command shell, run **edit buildroom** and enter the following code:

buildroom

```
1. --[[Room Building program by Al Sweigart
2. Builds a room of four walls.]]
3.
4. os.loadAPI('hare')
5.
6. -- handle command line arguments
7. local cliArgs = {...}
8. local length = tonumber(cliArgs[1])
9. local width = tonumber(cliArgs[2])
10. local height = tonumber(cliArgs[3])
11.
12. if length == nil or width == nil or height == nil or cliArgs[1] == '?' then
13.   print('Usage: buildroom <length> <width> <height>')
14.   return
15. end
16.
17. print('Building...')
18. if hare.buildRoom(length, width, height) == false then
19.   error('Not enough blocks.')
20. end
21. print('Done.')
```

After you've entered all of these instructions, save the program and exit the editor. You'll also need the `hare` module, which you can download by running `pastebin get wwzvaKuW hare`.

Like the `buildwall` program, the `buildroom` program relies mostly on a function in the `hare` module. First, it gathers the command line arguments from {...}, displaying a usage message if needed, and then it calls `hare.buildRoom()`. It's almost identical to the `buildwall` program except that we use the `hare.buildRoom()` function instead of `hare.buildWall()`.

RUNNING THE BUILDROOM PROGRAM

After placing the turtle and putting 72 stone brick blocks (or any other kind of building block) into its inventory, right-click the turtle to open its GUI. From the command shell, run **buildroom 5 6 4** to watch the turtle build a room five blocks long, six blocks wide, and four blocks high.

With the `buildwall` and `buildroom` programs, you can quickly build tall castles or other structures without ever placing a single block! You can craft multiple turtles running either the `buildRoom` program or the `buildWall` program to build structures in parallel, as shown in Figure 12-7.

Figure 12-7: Turtles constructing a castle by running the buildwall and buildroom programs

If you get errors when running this program, carefully compare your code to the code in this book to find any typos. If you still cannot fix your program, delete the file by running `delete buildroom` and then download it by running `pastebin get UOWVM4wg buildroom`.

WHAT YOU LEARNED

Although there were no programming concepts to learn in this chapter, it was good practice for developing algorithms. The more experience you get turning vague ideas of what you want the turtle to do into actual code, the better a programmer you'll be.

You created a wall-building function in Chapter 11 and a room-building function in this chapter. In Chapter 13, you'll develop an algorithm to build floors and ceilings.

CONSTRUCTING FLOORS

The rooms we built with the `buildRoom()` function in Chapter 12 are useful, but they won't keep the rain out. In this chapter, we'll write a `buildFloor()` function to build floors and ceilings, and we'll also write a `buildfloor` program to call that function. We'll use one function to build floors and ceilings because a ceiling is just a floor built higher up, as shown in Figure 13-1.

The algorithm we'll use to build floors will move a turtle across a rectangular area and make the turtle perform an action at every space. In this chapter, the turtle will place a block at every space in the rectangular area, but this flexible algorithm can perform many tasks. For example, in Chapter 14 we'll use this algorithm to write a farm program that plants seeds at every space in a rectangular area. Using a flexible algorithm instead of hardcoded solutions allows you to use the same code to solve a variety of problems!

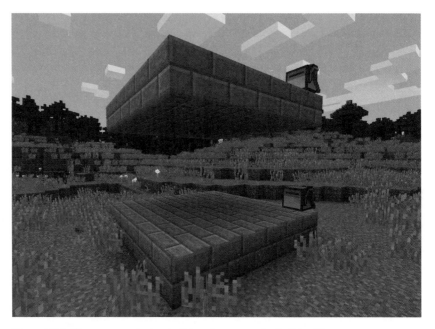

Figure 13-1: The same code that builds a floor can also build ceilings.

DESIGNING THE SWEEPING ALGORITHM

Building a horizontal surface is like building a wall, but instead of moving up after laying out a row of blocks, the turtle will move left or right to the next column. We'll call the turtle's action of moving across every space of a rectangular area *sweeping*, and we'll call the rectangular area the *field*.

We'll write the sweepField() function using an algorithm that has three parameters: length, width, and sweepFunc. The length and width parameters determine the size of the field, as shown in Figure 13-2.

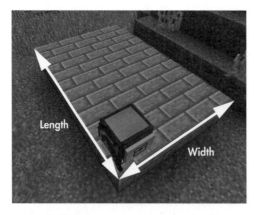

Figure 13-2: The length parameter is the distance in front of the turtle. The width parameter is the distance to the right of the turtle.

The sweepFunc parameter takes a function, which it calls at each space on the field. In the Lua programming language, we can pass functions for parameters, just like values. When the buildFloor() function uses sweepField() to build a floor, it passes a function that places blocks each time the turtle moves to a new space. Because sweepFunc is a parameter and we can pass other functions to it, we can customize sweepField() to instruct the turtle to perform any action we'd like. The focus of this chapter is creating floors, so we'll examine the algorithm as it's used in the buildfloor program.

BUILDING THE FLOOR

The buildfloor program will take two command line arguments: length and width. As mentioned earlier, these arguments determine how large the floor will be.

Figure 13-3 shows a top-down view of the path that a turtle will take to lay out a 3 × 4 floor.

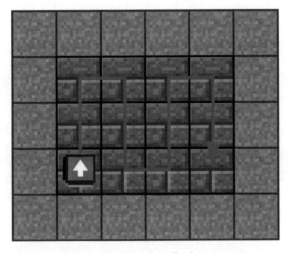

Figure 13-3: The path the turtle will take to sweep a rectangular 3 × 4 floor

To create the floor, the turtle will first move forward along the first column and call a function over each space to place a stone brick under itself. To tell the turtle which function to call, we'll use the sweepFunc parameter, which we'll look at in more detail in "Calling the sweepFunc() Function" on page 161. For now, just know that this parameter takes a function that will be called every time the turtle moves to a different position on the rectangular floor. In the buildfloor program, the function passed to sweepFunc is selectAndPlaceDown, which is the function in the hare module that selects the turtle's next nonempty inventory slot and places the selected block under the turtle. Because the turtle starts at the bottom-left corner, it only needs to move forward length - 1 times as it moves along the first column. This puts the turtle over the last block of the first column, as shown in Figure 13-4.

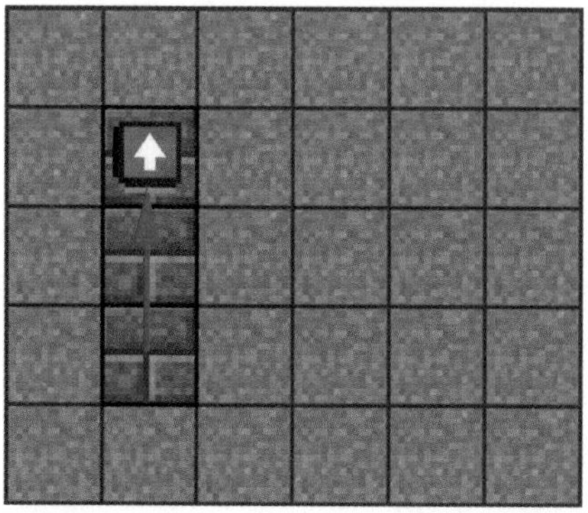

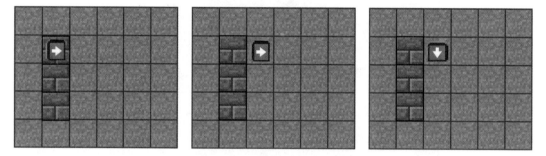

Figure 13-4: After moving forward `length - 1` times, the turtle is over the last block of the first column.

To move to the next column and face the correct direction, the turtle must turn right, move forward once, and then turn right again so it will end up in the position shown in Figure 13-5.

Figure 13-5: The turtle turns right, moves forward, and turns right again to prepare to build the next column.

Now the turtle runs similar code to travel along the next column. It moves forward `length - 1` times, calling selectAndPlaceDown at each space to place a block under itself. The result is that there are now two columns of blocks, as shown in Figure 13-6.

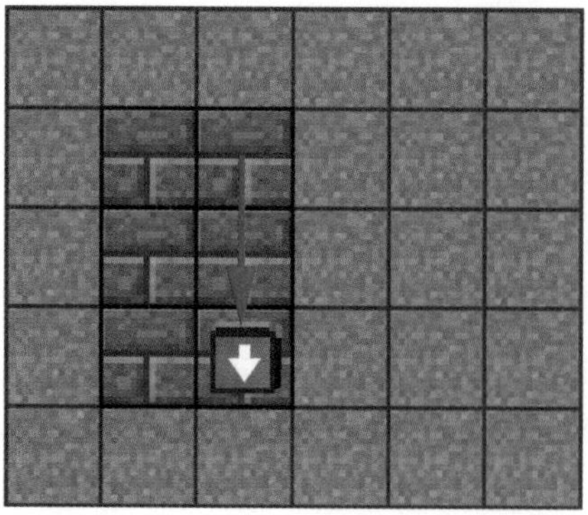

Figure 13-6: The turtle's position after finishing the second column

At this point, the turtle must turn left, move forward, and turn left again to move to the next column, as shown in Figure 13-7.

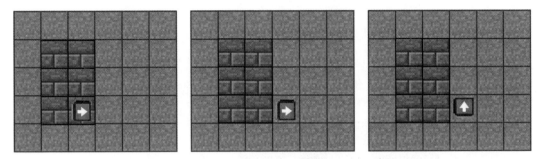

Figure 13-7: After the second column is built, the turtle must turn left, move forward, and then turn left again.

The turtle continues moving back and forth along the columns until the number of columns the turtle has completed equals the `width` of the field. When the turtle is done with this part of the algorithm, it will have created the floor, but its work won't be finished yet! We might want to run the `buildroom` program after the `buildfloor` program to create a room. In this case, we need the turtle to be in the same position and facing the same direction as when it began building the floor. Returning the turtle to its starting position ensures that the walls it builds when we call the `buildroom` program will align above the floor.

RETURNING TO THE STARTING POSITION

Making the turtle return to its starting position and face its starting direction after sweeping the entire field requires one of two different series of steps, depending on whether the width of the field is even or odd.

If the width is even, the turtle will be on the rightmost block of the bottom row of the floor, as shown in Figure 13-8.

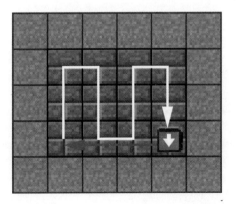

Figure 13-8: The turtle is at the rightmost block of the bottom row when the field's width is even.

The red line in Figure 13-8 shows the path the turtle must take to return to its starting space and face its starting direction. In this case, the turtle must:

1. Turn right
2. Move forward `width - 1` spaces
3. Turn right

However, if the field's width is odd, the turtle ends up at the top of the field when it's done placing all the blocks, as shown in Figure 13-9.

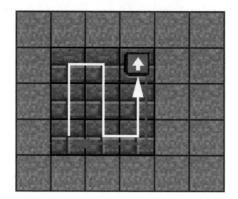

Figure 13-9: The turtle is at the rightmost block of the top row when the field's width is odd.

The red line in Figure 13-9 shows the path the turtle must take to return to its starting space and face its starting direction. In this case, the turtle must:

1. Move back `length - 1` spaces
2. Turn left
3. Move forward `width - 1` spaces
4. Turn right

You'll program this return behavior in the `sweepField()` function, but before you learn how to program the `sweepField()` function, you need to understand how to pass a function to another function.

PASSING FUNCTIONS TO FUNCTIONS

The `buildWall()` and `buildRoom()` functions we used in Chapters 11 and 12, respectively, are flexible and can build walls and rooms of any size because they use parameters for the `length`, `width`, and `height`. These parameters allow the functions to make walls and rooms of many different sizes without having to change the source code.

In this chapter, we'll add the `sweepField()` function to the `hare` module and call the `sweepField()` function in the `buildFloor` program. Currently, the `sweepField()` function moves the turtle to sweep over a rectangular field, placing a stone brick beneath itself at each space.

But we can also change the `sweepField()` function to make the turtle sweep over a rectangular farm to plant seeds and pick up wheat, or we can command the turtle to dig beneath itself to mine a rectangular hole in the ground. The code that makes the turtle move in the sweeping pattern remains the same, but the turtle's action can change at each space.

The `sweepField()` function has this flexibility because its `sweepFunc` parameter is passed a function that it calls as the turtle travels to each space in the rectangular field. In Lua, you can pass functions as arguments, just like you can pass integers or strings. Let's create a simple example program that passes a function for another function's parameter. In the command shell, enter **edit announce** to start a new program, and then enter the following:

announce

```
 1. function hello()
 2.   print('Hello there!')
 3. end
 4.
 5. function goodbye()
 6.   print('Goodbye!')
 7. end
 8.
 9. function announce(func)
10.   print('About to call the function.')
11.   func()
12.   print('Function called.')
13. end
14.
15. announce(hello)   -- no parentheses after hello
16. announce(goodbye)  -- no parentheses after goodbye
```

After you've entered all of these instructions, save the program and exit the editor. You can also download this program by running pastebin get sML2CbZ3 announce.

When you run this program from the command shell, you'll see this output:

```
> announce
About to call the function.
Hello there!
Function called.
About to call the function.
Goodbye!
Function called.
```

The `announce()` function has a single parameter called `func`. The first time `announce()` is called, on line 15, it is passed the `hello()` function for the parameter. Notice that the parentheses are not included after `hello`. The parentheses tell Lua to "call this function," but without the parentheses, Lua instead passes the `hello()` function to the `func` parameter in `announce()`. The `hello()` function is stored in the `func` parameter, just like an integer or string would be stored in a parameter. Then, on line 11, the function stored inside func is called because it has parentheses: func(). Because hello was passed for the func parameter, the hello() function is called, and the program displays Hello there!.

Later, line 16 will call the announce() function, but this time it will pass goodbye for the func parameter. So, when func() is called on line 11, the code inside the goodbye() function will run and print Goodbye!.

The code in the announce() function hasn't changed. It just knows that it should call whatever function is passed for its func parameter. Similarly, the sweepField() function we'll create will call the function passed for its sweepFunc parameter. The buildFloor() function will pass hare.selectAndPlaceDown to sweepField(), making it place blocks beneath the turtle at each space in the rectangular field.

EXTENDING THE HARE MODULE

Because the sweepField() function will be useful to many different programs, we'll put it in the hare module that we started in Chapter 7. The buildFloor() function, which we'll also add to the hare module, will call sweepField(). From the command shell, run **edit hare**. Move the cursor to the bottom of the file and continue the code by entering the following:

hare

```
...snip...
134. -- sweepField() moves across the rows
135. -- and columns of an area in front and
136. -- to the right of the turtle, calling
137. -- the provided sweepFunc at each space
138. function sweepField(length, width, sweepFunc)
139.    local turnRightNext = true
140.
141.    for x = 1, width do
142.       for y = 1, length do
143.          sweepFunc()
144.
145.          -- don't move forward on the last row
146.          if y ~= length then
147.             turtle.forward()
148.          end
149.       end
150.
151.       -- don't turn on the last column
152.       if x ~= width then
153.          -- turn to the next column
154.          if turnRightNext then
155.             turtle.turnRight()
156.             turtle.forward()
157.             turtle.turnRight()
158.          else
159.             turtle.turnLeft()
160.             turtle.forward()
161.             turtle.turnLeft()
162.          end
```

```
163.
164.        turnRightNext = not turnRightNext
165.      end
166.    end
167.
168.    -- move back to the start position
169.    if width % 2 == 0 then
170.      turtle.turnRight()
171.    else
172.      for y = 1, length - 1 do
173.        turtle.back()
174.      end
175.      turtle.turnLeft()
176.    end
177.
178.    for x = 1, width - 1 do
179.      turtle.forward()
180.    end
181.    turtle.turnRight()
182.
183.    return true
184. end
185.
186.
187. -- buildFloor() builds a rectangular
188. -- floor out of the blocks in the
189. -- inventory
190. function buildFloor(length, width)
191.    if countInventory() < length * width then
192.      return false  -- not enough blocks
193.    end
194.
195.    turtle.up()
196.    sweepField(length, width, selectAndPlaceDown)
197. end
```

After you've entered all of these instructions, save the program and exit the editor. You can also download this module by running pastebin get wwzvaKuW hare.

CALLING THE SWEEPFUNC() FUNCTION

Let's look at the new hare functions one at a time, starting with sweepField(). All the sweepField() function does is move the turtle across the entire field, calling a function passed in as a parameter once at each space. The length and width parameters tell sweepField() how many rows long and how many columns wide the field is, respectively.

To run sweepFunc() at each space the turtle moves to, we use one for loop to iterate over each column and another for loop to iterate over each row.

hare
```
134. -- sweepField() moves across the rows
135. -- and columns of an area in front and
```

```
136.  -- to the right of the turtle, calling
137.  -- the provided sweepFunc at each space
138.  function sweepField(length, width, sweepFunc)
139.    local turnRightNext = true
140.
141.    for x = 1, width do
142.      for y = 1, length do
143.        sweepFunc()
```

At the end of each column, the turtle alternates between turning to the right and turning to the left, so line 139 sets the turnRightNext variable to true.

The two nested for loops iterate to keep track of which column and row the turtle is on. The x variable keeps track of which column the turtle is on, and the y variable keeps track of which row the turtle is on. When y is equal to length, the turtle is on the last row of its current column. When x is equal to width, the turtle is on the last column of its current row. Figure 13-10 shows the value of x and y at each block as the turtle sweeps the field. Notice that the y value starts at 1 on different sides because the turtle alternates between moving up and down columns.

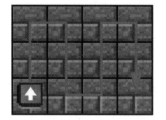

| x = 1 | x = 2 | x = 3 | x = 4 |
y = 3	y = 1	y = 3	y = 1
x = 1	x = 2	x = 3	x = 4
y = 2	y = 2	y = 2	y = 2
x = 1	x = 2	x = 3	x = 4
y = 1	y = 3	y = 1	y = 3

Figure 13-10: The path the turtle moves as it sweeps the field (left) and the values of the x and y variables at each space (right)

Inside the inner for loop, line 143 calls sweepFunc(). Remember that sweepFunc is a parameter, not the name of a function. There is no function sweepFunc() line anywhere in our programs to define a function of that name. Instead, sweepFunc is a parameter that we will set to a function. As a result, any function can be passed to sweepField() and it will be called on line 143 as sweepFunc().

MOVING ALONG THE ROWS AND COLUMNS

After calling sweepFunc(), the turtle needs to move to the next space. The inner for loop that begins on 142 iterates the y variable from 1 to length. The turtle needs to move up or down length - 1 rows for each column, so lines 146 to 148 call turtle.forward() on each iteration of the for loop except for the last iteration (when y will be equal to length).

```
hare   145.      -- don't move forward on the last row
       146.      if y ~= length then
       147.        turtle.forward()
       148.      end
       149.    end
```

When the program reaches line 149 and the for loop that started on line 142 finishes, the turtle has reached the last row and the end of the column. If the turtle isn't yet on the last column (you can tell because x will be equal to width), the turtle needs to move the next column.

The direction the turtle needs to turn in order to move to the next column depends on whether turnRightNext is true or false. (See Figures 13-5 and 13-7 for the different turns the turtle must make.) If turnRightNext is true, lines 155 to 157 make the turtle turn to the right, move forward, and turn to the right again. If turnRightNext is false, lines 159 to 161 make the turtle turn to the left, move forward, and turn to the left again. Either way, the turtle will be at the start of the next column.

```
151.    -- don't turn on the last column
152.    if x ~= width then
153.        -- turn to the next column
154.        if turnRightNext then
155.            turtle.turnRight()
156.            turtle.forward()
157.            turtle.turnRight()
158.        else
159.            turtle.turnLeft()
160.            turtle.forward()
161.            turtle.turnLeft()
162.        end
163.
164.        turnRightNext = not turnRightNext
165.    end
166. end
```

The next time the turtle must turn to the next column, it will have to turn in the other direction, so line 164 toggles the Boolean value in turnRightNext. The end statement on line 165 ends the if statement on line 152, and the end statement on line 166 ends the for loop on line 141. When the execution gets past line 166, the turtle has swept the entire field and is ready to return to the starting space.

FIGURING OUT IF A NUMBER IS EVEN OR ODD WITH THE MODULUS OPERATOR

The turtle must take two different paths to return to its starting space after it finishes sweeping the field. Recall that these paths were shown in Figures 13-8 and 13-9 and that which path the turtle takes depends on whether the field's width is even or odd. To determine whether a number is even or odd, we need to check whether the number is divisible by 2. When a number is divisible by 2, it's even. When a number is not divisible by 2 and leaves a remainder of 1, the number is odd.

Therefore, to determine whether a number is even or odd, we just need to find the remainder when we divide the number by two. We can do this by using the *modulus operator*, or *mod operator* (%). (This name isn't related to Minecraft mods.)

Enter the following into the Lua shell to see how the mod operator works:

```
lua> 6 % 2
0
lua> 7 % 2
1
lua> 8 % 2
0
```

We use the mod operator like we use the division operator (/): enter the number to divide, the % operator, and the number to divide by (which in this case is 2). Even numbers modded by 2 will always result in 0 because even numbers leave no remainder when divided by 2. Odd numbers modded by 2 will always result in 1.

Using this mod trick, we can determine whether width is an even or odd number.

THE EVEN-WIDTH AND ODD-WIDTH PATHS

The path the turtle must take to return to the starting space differs depending on whether width is even or odd, so we'll use an if statement.

```
hare    168.    -- move back to the start position
        169.    if width % 2 == 0 then
        170.      turtle.turnRight()
        171.    else
        172.      for y = 1, length - 1 do
        173.        turtle.back()
        174.      end
        175.      turtle.turnLeft()
        176.    end
```

If the width of the field is an even number, then width % 2 will be equal to 0 and the condition for the if statement on line 169 will be true. In that case, line 170 turns the turtle to the right. Otherwise, if the width is odd, lines 172 to 174 move the turtle backward to the other end of the row, and line 175 turns the turtle to the left. In both cases, the turtle will end up at the start of the column, facing left.

Next, lines 178 to 180 move the turtle forward width - 1 spaces to return the turtle to its starting position. To make the turtle face its starting direction, line 181 turns the turtle to the right.

```
hare    178.    for x = 1, width - 1 do
        179.      turtle.forward()
        180.    end
        181.    turtle.turnRight()
        182.
        183.    return true
        184. end
```

At this point, the turtle is back at its starting position, so line 183 returns true. The end statement on line 184 ends the sweepField() function's code block.

Remember, the sweepField() function isn't written specifically to build a floor. Instead, we can use the function for many different purposes because it makes a turtle sweep a field while calling a function at each space. To make floors, we'll create the buildFloor() function.

WRITING THE BUILDFLOOR() FUNCTION

Using the sweepField() function, the buildFloor() function builds a rectangular floor using the blocks in the turtle's inventory. The buildFloor() function takes length and width variables as arguments to specify how large the floor should be.

hare

```
187. -- buildFloor() builds a rectangular
188. -- floor out of the blocks in the
189. -- inventory
190. function buildFloor(length, width)
191.   if countInventory() < length * width then
192.     return false  -- not enough blocks
193.   end
```

Line 191 calls countInventory() and compares the number of blocks in the turtle's inventory to the number of blocks needed to create a floor. A floor that is length blocks long and width blocks wide will require length * width blocks to build. If the turtle doesn't have enough blocks to build a floor, the function will end.

If the turtle has enough blocks, line 195 moves the turtle up once so the turtle can place the floor blocks underneath itself as it sweeps the field.

hare

```
195.   turtle.up()
196.   sweepField(length, width, selectAndPlaceDown)
197. end
```

Line 196 passes the length, width, and the selectAndPlaceDown function to sweepField(). The call on line 196 tells sweepField() to call the function selectAndPlaceDown() at each space in the field so the turtle places blocks to build the floor.

That's it for the buildFloor() function. This function is short because most of the work is done by the sweepField() function.

WRITING THE BUILDFLOOR PROGRAM

We put the buildFloor() and sweepField() functions in the hare module so programs can call the functions, but it would still be useful to have a program just for building floors. Just like the buildwall and buildroom programs in

Chapters 11 and 12, the buildfloor program will accept command line arguments, provide a usage message, and call hare.buildFloor() to construct the floor or ceiling.

From the command shell, run **edit buildfloor** and enter the following code:

buildfloor

```
1. --[[Floor Building program by Al Sweigart
2. Builds a rectangular floor.]]
3.
4. os.loadAPI('hare')
5.
6. -- handle command line arguments
7. local cliArgs = {...}
8. local length = tonumber(cliArgs[1])
9. local width = tonumber(cliArgs[2])
10.
11. if length == nil or width == nil or cliArgs[1] == '?' then
12.    print('Usage: buildwall <length> <width>')
13.    return
14. end
15.
16. hare.buildFloor(length, width)
```

After you've entered all of these instructions, save the program and exit the editor.

Because buildfloor is so similar to the buildwall and buildroom programs, I won't explain the code again. The program simply takes command line arguments to determine the length and width of the floor, which the hare .buildFloor() function passes to sweepField().

RUNNING THE BUILDFLOOR PROGRAM

After placing the turtle, right-click the turtle to open its GUI. Load at least 30 stone bricks (or some other building block) into its inventory. From the command shell, run **buildfloor 5 6** to watch the turtle build a floor five blocks long and six blocks wide.

After that, you can run buildroom 5 6 4 to build the walls for a room above the floor. And when this room is finished, turning the turtle to the right and running buildfloor 5 6 again will build a flat roof for this room! Now you have everything you need to build rectangular rooms.

If you get errors when running this program, carefully compare your code to the code in this book to find any typos. If you still cannot fix your program, delete the file by running delete buildfloor and then download it by running pastebin get Epr9CndN buildfloor.

CREATING A PATTERNED FLOOR

As mentioned earlier, because the sweepField() function lets us pass any function for its sweepFunc parameter, it's very flexible. Let's write a buildcheckerboard program that builds a checkered floor using coal blocks and quartz blocks.

You can craft coal blocks from nine pieces of coal, and you can craft quartz blocks from four pieces of quartz. Figure 13-11 shows these recipes. Note that you can only mine Nether quartz from the Nether (see *http://minecraft.gamepedia.com/The_Nether*).

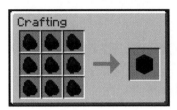 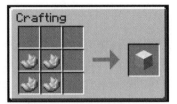

Figure 13-11: Crafting coal blocks (left) and quartz blocks (right)

Because we're already making a checkered floor, let's make the floor into a checkerboard so you can play checkers with your turtles in Minecraft!

WRITING THE BUILDCHECKERBOARD PROGRAM

To make an 8 × 8 checkerboard, we'll need to collect 32 coal blocks and 32 quartz blocks. After we create the buildcheckerboard program, we'll modify the turtle's colors so you'll be able to create an 8 × 8 checkerboard. From the command shell, run **edit buildcheckerboard** and enter the following code:

build checkerboard

```
1. --[[Checkerboard Building program by Al Sweigart
2. Builds a checkerboard floor.]]
3.
4. os.loadAPI('hare')
5.
6. -- handle command line arguments
7. local cliArgs = {...}
8. local length = tonumber(cliArgs[1])
9. local width = tonumber(cliArgs[2])
10.
11. if length == nil or width == nil or cliArgs[1] == '?' then
12.   print('Usage: buildcheckerboard <length> <width>')
13.   return
14. end
15.
16. local placeBlack = true
17.
18. function placeCheckerboard()
19.   -- select coal or quartz, based on placeBlack
20.   if placeBlack then
21.     hare.selectItem('minecraft:coal_block')
22.   else
23.     hare.selectItem('minecraft:quartz_block')
24.   end
25.
26.   turtle.placeDown()
27.   placeBlack = not placeBlack
28. end
```

```
29.
30. turtle.up()
31. hare.sweepField(length, width, placeCheckerboard)
```

After you've entered all of these instructions, save the program and exit the editor.

RUNNING THE BUILDCHECKERBOARD PROGRAM

Place the 32 coal blocks and 32 quartz blocks into the turtle's inventory, and then run **buildcheckerboard 8 8** from the command shell. The turtle will start creating an 8 × 8 checkerboard floor, which you can see in Figure 13-12.

Figure 13-12: The turtle in the process of making the checkerboard floor

If you get errors when running this program, carefully compare your code to the code in this book to find any typos. If you still cannot fix your program, delete the file by running delete buildcheckerboard and then download it by running pastebin get QQQK3mqk buildcheckerboard.

Although we made the buildCheckerboard program to make a checkered floor the size of a standard-sized checkerboard, you can actually create checkered floors of any size now. These can be part of a fancy castle floor, as shown in Figure 13-13.

Figure 13-13: A turtle-built checkered floor in a turtle-built castle

Or, if you create 24 turtles and hold either rose red dye or bone meal while right-clicking the turtles to dye them red or white, respectively, you can create a checkers set, as shown in Figure 13-14.

Figure 13-14: A checkerboard of turtles

Even building a giant 32 × 32 checkered floor, as shown in Figure 13-15, is easy when a turtle makes it for you.

Figure 13-15: A turtle-built 32 × 32 checkered floor

WRITING THE PLACECHECKERBOARD() FUNCTION

Unlike the `hare.selectAndPlaceDown()` function, which simply selects any slot with items in it before placing a block down, the `placeCheckerboard()` function looks at the `placeBlack` variable to determine whether to select a coal block or a quartz block.

The placeBlack variable is first created with a local statement on line 16, outside of all functions.

build checkerboard

```
16. local placeBlack = true
```

The placeCheckerboard() function checks if this variable is true or false to decide which block the turtle should select.

build checkerboard

```
18. function placeCheckerboard()
19.    -- select coal or quartz, based on placeBlack
20.    if placeBlack then
21.      hare.selectItem('minecraft:coal_block')
22.    else
23.      hare.selectItem('minecraft:quartz_block')
24.    end
25.
26.    turtle.placeDown()
```

When placeBlack is true, the program calls hare.selectItem() to select an inventory slot containing coal blocks. When placeBlack is false, the program instead selects an inventory slot containing quartz blocks.

After the if and else statements specify which block type to select with the hare.selectItem() function, line 26 places the selected block type below the turtle.

Then line 27 toggles the Boolean value stored in placeBlack.

build checkerboard

```
27.    placeBlack = not placeBlack
28. end
```

If placeBlack was true, now it will be false. If placeBlack was false, now it will be true. This means that the next time placeCheckerboard() is called by the sweepField() function, the opposite-color block will be placed. This code produces the checkered pattern.

CALLING THE SWEEPFIELD() FUNCTION

After the placeCheckerboard() function ends on line 28, the main part of the program continues. Line 30 moves the turtle up one space so it has room to place blocks below it.

build checkerboard

```
30. turtle.up()
31. hare.sweepField(length, width, placeCheckerboard)
```

It then calls hare.sweepField(), passing in the command line arguments as length and width. It also passes in the placeCheckerboard function as a value, which has no parentheses after it because the program isn't calling the placeCheckerboard() function but is rather passing in the function.

WHAT YOU LEARNED

In this chapter, we created a generic sweep field algorithm that has the turtle visit each space in a rectangle and perform an action. The buildfloor program uses this algorithm to build floors and ceilings, but you can apply the algorithm to many different kinds of tasks. This is possible because Lua lets you pass functions to other functions just as easily as you pass string or integer values. When the selectAndPlaceDown() function was passed to sweepField() in the buildfloor program, the turtle built a floor. But when the more specialized placeCheckerboard() function was passed to sweepField() in the buildCheckerboard program, the turtle built a checkered floor.

Because the sweepField() function is so adaptable, it doesn't take much additional code to program new behaviors. In Chapter 14, we'll use the sweepField() function to create an automated farm to do all your planting and harvesting chores for you.

PROGRAMMING A
ROBOTIC FARM

In Survival mode, you need to make sure you're fed, but hunting for and gathering food is time consuming. Farming and stocking food are better solutions, but maintaining a large farm can be quite a chore. However, you can manage a giant crop field with one well-programmed farming turtle, as shown in Figure 14-1.

Figure 14-1: One turtle can work a large-scale wheat farm.

In this chapter, you'll write an algorithm that tells your turtles how to plant, harvest, and store crops.

SETTING UP A WHEAT FIELD

To create a wheat-farming algorithm, you must understand how to make a wheat field in Minecraft. To do this, you'll need a hoe, a flat area of dirt or grass blocks, a bucket, access to a water source such as an ocean or river (the water source doesn't need to be near the grass), fence blocks, and a chest.

First, go to your water source with your empty bucket and right-click the water with the bucket to fill it. Then, go to your flat area of dirt or grass blocks and use a hoe to till the top of the flat area until you have a 9 × 9 area of tilled blocks. Because tilled blocks revert back to dirt if water isn't nearby, you'll need to dig a hole in the middle of your 9 × 9 field and then right-click the hole with the water bucket. Doing so will fill the hole with water. This single water block can water all dirt blocks up to four blocks away from it in any direction, creating a 9 × 9 field for your farm. You can place many of these 9 × 9 fields next to each other to create larger farms.

You should also place a fence around the farm to keep out cows, sheep, and monsters that would block the turtle's path, and you should place a chest one block off the ground in the bottom-left corner of the farm for the turtle to store its harvest. Figure 14-2 shows what your field should look like.

NOTE   *A single turtle can manage a rectangular area of any size. Just be sure to have one water block for each 9 × 9 portion of the field to keep the crops irrigated. You need only one fence around the rectangular field (no matter its size) to keep out mobs and animals.*

Figure 14-2: A 9 × 9 wheat field with water in the middle and a turtle and chest in the bottom-left corner

Now that your farm is set up, let's look at the algorithm the farmwheat program uses to run the farm.

DESIGNING THE WHEAT-FARMING ALGORITHM

Later in this chapter, we'll write the farmwheat program, but first we need to plan the algorithm the program should use. Before the turtle can start farming the field, it needs to check two things. First, the turtle checks that it is starting next to a chest. If it can't find a chest, it has nowhere to drop the wheat that it harvests. Because the farmwheat program will reuse the hare.sweepField() function we wrote in Chapter 13, the turtle also needs to check that it has enough fuel to complete a sweep of the field.

After the turtle confirms that it has a chest next to it and enough fuel, it will use the hare.sweepField() function to move over the entire area of the field. Because wheat matures at different rates (most crops grow to maturity within 30 to 60 minutes, or two to three Minecraft days), the whole wheat field probably won't be mature at the same time. Therefore, we'll need to design a function to pass to hare.sweepField() that will determine what the turtle should do at each space in the field.

The turtle needs to perform one of three actions:

- Plant a seed if no wheat is planted in the space
- Do nothing if wheat is planted but hasn't matured yet
- Harvest the wheat if it is mature and plant a seed

After the turtle performs one of these three actions on each space, the turtle will return to its original position, which we programmed into the hare.sweepField() function in Chapter 13. In this case, the turtle's starting position is next to the chest. The turtle turns to face the chest, drops any harvested wheat into it, and then turns to face the field again. Then the turtle sleeps for 10 minutes to give the planted wheat time to mature before sweeping the field again.

Now that you understand how the algorithm works, you can use it to create the farmwheat program. We'll start by adding a helper function called findBlock() to hare, which the turtle will use to confirm that it is near a chest.

EXTENDING THE HARE MODULE

The findBlock() function causes the turtle to spin around to see if a certain block is nearby. This function will help our farming turtle locate a nearby chest for storing the harvested wheat. We'll add the findBlock() function to the hare module because it will also be useful to other programs.

From the command shell, run **edit hare**. Move the cursor to the bottom of the file and continue the code by adding the following lines:

hare

```
    ...snip...
200. -- findBlock() spins around searching
201. -- for the named block next to the turtle
202. function findBlock(name)
203.    local result, block
204.
205.    for i = 1, 4 do
206.       result, block = turtle.inspect()
207.       if block ~= nil and block['name'] == name then
208.          return true
209.       end
210.       turtle.turnRight()
211.    end
212.    return false
213. end
```

After you've entered all of these instructions, save and exit the editor. You can also download this program by running pastebin get wwzvaKuW hare.

The findBlock() function is very simple to use. You pass findBlock() a string for the name ID of the block you're looking for. For example, later on we'll pass the function the name ID 'minecraft:chest' to search for a chest. The findBlock() function causes the turtle to turn right up to four times using the for loop on line 205 and has the turtle inspect the block currently in front of it at each turn by using the turtle.inspect() function.

The turtle.inspect() function returns two values. It returns the value true if a block is in front of the turtle to inspect or false if a block is not there. When there is a block to inspect, the turtle also returns data about the block. On line 206, we store the boolean returned from turtle. inspect() in the variable result, and we store the block data in the variable block. Every time the turtle inspects, it checks whether a block exists and whether the block has the same name ID as the one passed to findBlock(). If the turtle finds the block it's looking for, it stops turning and returns true. Otherwise, the turtle continues turning until it turns a total of four times. If the turtle doesn't find the block it's looking for after four turns, the findBlock() function returns false. With our helper function ready, we can start coding the main farmwheat program.

WRITING THE FARMWHEAT PROGRAM

Let's implement the farming algorithm. From the command shell, run **edit farmwheat** and enter the following code:

farmwheat

```
1. --[[Wheat Farming program by Al Sweigart
2. Plants and harvests wheat.
3. Assumes a field is in front and
4. to the right of the turtle,
5. with a chest behind it.]]
6.
7. os.loadAPI('hare')
8.
9. -- handle command line arguments
10. local cliArgs = {...}
11. local length = tonumber(cliArgs[1])
12. local width = tonumber(cliArgs[2])
13.
14. -- display "usage" info
15. if length == nil or width == nil or cliArgs[1] == '?' then
16.   print('Usage: farmwheat <length> <width>')
17.   return
18. end
19.
20. print('Hold Ctrl-T to stop.')
21.
22. -- check that chest is there
23. if not hare.findBlock('minecraft:chest') then
24.   error('Must start next to a chest.')
25. end
26.
27. -- face field
28. turtle.turnLeft()
29. turtle.turnLeft()
30.
31.
32. -- checkWheatCrop() harvests mature wheat
33. -- and plants seeds
34. function checkWheatCrop()
35.   local result, block = turtle.inspectDown()
```

```
36.
37.   if not result then
38.     turtle.digDown()  -- till the soil
39.     plantWheatSeed()
40.   elseif block ~= nil and block['name'] == 'minecraft:wheat' and
          block['metadata'] == 7 then
41.     -- collect wheat and replant
42.     turtle.digDown()
43.     print('Collected wheat.')
44.     plantWheatSeed()
45.   end
46. end
47.
48.
49. -- plantWheatSeed() attempts to plant
50. -- a wheat seed below the turtle
51. function plantWheatSeed()
52.   if not hare.selectItem('minecraft:wheat_seeds') then
53.     print('Warning: Low on seeds.')
54.   else
55.     turtle.placeDown()  -- plant a seed
56.     print('Planted seed.')
57.   end
58. end
59.
60.
61. -- storeWheat() puts all wheat into an
62. -- adjacent chest
63. function storeWheat()
64.   -- face the chest
65.   if not hare.findBlock('minecraft:chest') then
66.     error('Could not find chest.')
67.   end
68.
69.   -- store wheat in chest
70.   while hare.selectItem('minecraft:wheat') do
71.     print('Dropping off ' .. turtle.getItemCount() .. ' wheat...')
72.     if not turtle.drop() then
73.       error('Wheat chest is full!')
74.     end
75.   end
76.
77.   -- face field again
78.   turtle.turnLeft()
79.   turtle.turnLeft()
80. end
81.
82.
83. -- begin farming
84. while true do
85.   -- check fuel
86.   if turtle.getFuelLevel() < (length * width + length + width) then
87.     error('Turtle needs more fuel!')
88.   end
```

```
89.
90.    -- farm wheat
91.    print('Sweeping field...')
92.    hare.sweepField(length, width, checkWheatCrop)
93.    storeWheat()
94.
95.    print('Sleeping for 10 minutes...')
96.    os.sleep(600)
97. end
```

After you've entered all of these instructions, save and exit the editor.

RUNNING THE FARMWHEAT PROGRAM

To run the farmwheat program, you must make sure water is within four blocks of each dirt block in the field and that a chest is behind the turtle's starting space in the bottom-left corner of the field, as shown in Figure 14-3. You also equip the turtle with a diamond hoe so it can till the dirt or grass blocks. After the turtle is set up, enter **farmwheat 9 9** into the command shell to have the turtle farm a 9 × 9 field.

Figure 14-3: The turtle must start one block above the ground with a chest behind it.

Keep in mind that if you move too far away from the turtle, the turtle shuts down. If the turtle shuts down in the middle of the wheat field, you'll need to move the turtle back to the bottom-left corner of the field and run the program again to make the turtle continue farming. The turtle will continue sweeping over the field, checking and planting wheat as before.

If you get errors when running this program, carefully compare your code to the code in this book to find any typos. If you still cannot fix your program, delete the file by running delete farmwheat and then download it by running pastebin get SfcB8b55 farmwheat.

SETUP FOR THE FARMWHEAT PROGRAM

The first five lines of the program consist of the usual comments that describe who wrote the program and what it does. Line 7 loads the hare module so the program can call its functions.

Then the program reads in the command line arguments to get the length and width of the wheat field. If the command line arguments aren't provided, the program displays a usage message.

farmwheat

```
 9. -- handle command line arguments
10. local cliArgs = {...}
11. local length = tonumber(cliArgs[1])
12. local width = tonumber(cliArgs[2])
13.
14. -- display "usage" info
15. if length == nil or width == nil or cliArgs[1] == '?' then
16.   print('Usage: farmwheat <length> <width>')
17.   return
18. end
```

Because command line arguments are always strings but the length and width variables will always contain numbers, lines 11 and 12 pass the first and second command line arguments to the tonumber() function. The return values are stored in length and width.

If there is no first or second command line argument, tonumber() will return nil to store in length or width, respectively. When there is no second command line argument or if the first command line argument is '?', the condition for the if statement on line 15 will be true and lines 16 and 17 will execute. Line 16 displays the usage message, and the return statement on line 17 terminates the program.

Next, the program performs more setup steps to make sure the turtle has everything it needs to run the farmwheat program.

farmwheat

```
20. print('Hold Ctrl-T to stop.')
21.
22. -- check that chest is there
23. if not hare.findBlock('minecraft:chest') then
24.   error('Must start next to a chest.')
25. end
26.
27. -- face field
28. turtle.turnLeft()
29. turtle.turnLeft()
```

Line 20 displays a reminder to the user that they can terminate the program by holding down CTRL-T. The turtle then tries to find the chest with a call to hare.findBlock('minecraft:chest'). If it can't find a chest, line 24 terminates the program with an error message because there's no point in continuing the program if there is no chest to store the wheat in.

Because the chest is behind the turtle and the wheat field, the turtle needs to turn left twice (on lines 28 and 29) to face the field again.

WRITING FUNCTIONS TO USE IN THE MAIN PROGRAM

Let's write a function named checkWheatCrop() that tells the turtle what to do at each space on the field it sweeps, and let's write another function named plantWheatSeed() that contains the instructions to plant wheat seeds. We'll also write a third function named storeWheat() that instructs the turtle on what it should do after it finishes harvesting wheat. These three functions will be called from the main part of the farmwheat program.

CHECKING THE CROP

The checkWheatCrop() function inspects the space below the turtle and determines the action the turtle should take. We'll pass checkWheatCrop() to sweepField() so the function is called at each space the turtle goes over on the field.

The following code instructs the turtle to plant a seed if there currently is no wheat under the turtle.

farmwheat
```
32. -- checkWheatCrop() harvests mature wheat
33. -- and plants seeds
34. function checkWheatCrop()
35.   local result, block = turtle.inspectDown()
36.
37.   if not result then
38.     turtle.digDown()  -- till the soil
39.     plantWheatSeed()
```

The turtle.inspectDown() function has the turtle inspect the space directly under it. If there is no wheat, the result variable on line 35 is set to false and line 38 tills the dirt block. Line 39 calls plantWheatSeed(), which we'll create in the next section. The plantWheatSeed() function plants a wheat seed on the tilled soil block beneath the turtle.

If the space under the turtle isn't empty (that is, the space contains wheat or a seed), the turtle checks whether the space contains mature wheat.

farmwheat
```
40.   elseif block ~= nil and block['name'] == 'minecraft:wheat' and
          block['metadata'] == 7 then
41.     -- collect wheat and replant
42.     turtle.digDown()
43.     print('Collected wheat.')
44.     plantWheatSeed()
45.   end
46. end
```

Line 40 checks whether `block` is equal to the value `nil` and then checks whether the `block['name']` value is the same as a wheat block's ID name. If nothing was under the turtle, the `turtle.inspectDown()` call on line 35 would have set `block` to `nil`. This would cause `block['name']` on line 40 to be an error because `block` would be `nil` instead of a table value. This potential error is why line 40 first checks that `block` doesn't equal `nil`.

The table value in `block` also has a `'metadata'` key whose value indicates how much the wheat has grown. When the wheat seed has just been planted, the `'metadata'` value equals 0. When the value equals 7, the wheat has matured and the last condition on line 40 would be true.

In sum, line 40 checks for three different conditions: whether there is a block under the turtle, whether this block is a wheat block, and whether this wheat block has matured. If any of these conditions returns `false`, the execution moves to line 46, which is the end of the block, and the turtle does nothing.

If all the conditions on line 40 are true, line 42 harvests the wheat by calling `turtle.digDown()`. Whether mining ore, chopping wood, or harvesting wheat, the `turtle.dig()` functions use the turtle's equipped tool to collect blocks. Line 44 calls `plantWheatSeed()`, which replaces the wheat that the turtle just harvested. We'll examine this function next.

PLANTING SEEDS

Because we need the same wheat-planting code on lines 39 and 44, we put the code in its own `plantWheatSeed()` function to avoid having to enter it twice. When you write your own Lua programs, your programs will be more readable if you use functions to eliminate duplicate code.

The first task that the `plantWheatSeed()` function on line 51 performs is to select wheat seeds in the turtle's inventory by passing `'minecraft:wheat_seeds'` to the call to `hare.selectItem()` so the selected slot contains wheat seeds.

farmwheat

```
49. -- plantWheatSeed() attempts to plant
50. -- a wheat seed below the turtle
51. function plantWheatSeed()
52.   if not hare.selectItem('minecraft:wheat_seeds') then
53.     print('Warning: Low on seeds.')
```

If there are no seeds, the turtle displays a warning message, doesn't plant a seed, and continues on through the rest of the program. The program doesn't need to terminate because the turtle gets more seeds as it harvests mature wheat crops. But if the `selectItem()` call on line 52 returns `true`, the turtle's inventory will have seeds selected.

The `else` code block that starts on line 54 plants a seed and displays a message to the player.

farmwheat

```
54.   else
55.     turtle.placeDown()  -- plant a seed
56.     print('Planted seed.')
57.   end
58. end
```

On line 55, turtle.placeDown() plants a seed if seeds are in the current slot and tilled soil is under the turtle. Then, line 56 displays Planted seed. to the user, and line 58 ends the plantWheatSeed() function's code block.

STORING WHEAT

After the turtle sweeps the field, it needs to drop any harvested wheat into the chest. To do this, the program calls the storeWheat() function when the sweep has finished. This function makes the turtle first find and then face a chest.

farmwheat

```
61. -- storeWheat() puts all wheat into an
62. -- adjacent chest
63. function storeWheat()
64.   -- face the chest
65.   if not hare.findBlock('minecraft:chest') then
66.     error('Could not find chest.')
67.   end
```

Line 65 calls hare.findBlock() and passes it 'minecraft:chest', which causes the turtle to spin around, stopping when it finds a chest. If the turtle can't find a chest, the hare.findBlock() function call returns false and line 66 terminates the program with an error message.

Otherwise, the program continues and assumes the turtle is facing a chest. The turtle must select an inventory slot that contains wheat and drop it into the chest by calling turtle.drop().

farmwheat

```
69.   -- store wheat in chest
70.   while hare.selectItem('minecraft:wheat') do
71.     print('Dropping off ' .. turtle.getItemCount() .. ' wheat...')
72.     if not turtle.drop() then
73.       error('Wheat chest is full!')
74.     end
75.   end
```

Line 70 is a while loop whose condition is based on the value returned by hare.selectItem('minecraft:wheat'). As long as wheat is in the turtle's inventory, this function call returns true and the while loop continues to loop. Inside this loop, line 71 shows the player the number of wheat items in the current slot and line 72 attempts to drop them into the chest in front of the turtle.

If the chest is already full, the call to turtle.drop() on line 72 returns false. In this case, line 73 terminates the program with an error message. Otherwise, the loop keeps looping until there is no more wheat, and then the execution moves on to line 78.

When the turtle is facing the chest, the field is behind it. To face the field again, the turtle needs to turn around.

farmwheat

```
77.   -- face field again
78.   turtle.turnLeft()
79.   turtle.turnLeft()
80. end
```

Lines 78 and 79 turn the turtle to the left twice so that it is facing the field again. Line 80 ends the storeWheat() function.

We now have all three functions that will be called from the main program: checkWheatCrop(), plantWheatSeed(), and storeWheat(). Let's start farming!

FARMING WITH A LOOP

Let's write the main loop of the program with the functions defined on lines 32 to 80. In this loop, the turtle first checks that it has enough fuel. If the turtle has enough fuel to sweep the field it's on, it will plant and harvest the wheat field, store any harvested wheat in a chest, and then wait 10 minutes to allow the wheat to grow before repeating the whole process.

The loop's first step checks that the turtle has enough fuel to move across the entire field and back to the starting space.

farmwheat

```
83. -- begin farming
84. while true do
85.     -- check fuel
86.   if turtle.getFuelLevel() < (length * width + length + width) then
87.     error('Turtle needs more fuel!')
88.   end
```

On line 84, the while loop's condition is true. Therefore, the loop will loop forever, so the program terminates only if error() is called or the player holds down CTRL-T.

To check how much fuel a turtle needs, we need to come up with an equation to calculate the fuel units the turtle needs to sweep the field. To keep this calculation simple, we'll overestimate the turtle's fuel needs.

First, we figure out how many units of fuel the turtle needs to travel down each column. Turtles use one unit of fuel each time they move, and moving down one column that is length blocks long requires length - 1 moves, so that would be length - 1 units of fuel. However, the turtle also uses fuel whenever it moves to the next column of the field. So the turtle needs length - 1 + 1, or length, units of fuel to move along each column.

We then multiply the length number by the number of rows in the field. There are width number of rows in the field, so we'll calculate the total amount of fuel the turtle needs to sweep the entire field as length * width.

In addition, the turtle needs enough fuel to move back to its starting position. If the turtle ends up at the far end of the field from its starting position, it needs to move down one column (length number of moves) and down one row (width number of moves). So the final formula for the amount of fuel the turtle needs to do one sweep of the field is length * width + length + width. Figure 14-4 shows a diagram of the formula.

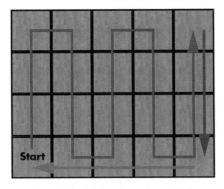

```
length * width + length + width
```

Figure 14-4: A diagram showing each part of the
*length * width + length + width calculation*

Of course, this formula is an overestimate because the turtle could end up on the closer side of the field, where it only needs to move down one row to get back to its starting position. Also, the leftmost path of the red arrow should be `length - 1` blocks long to account for the starting block, not `length` blocks long, and the blue arrow should be `length - 1` blocks long as well to account for the corner block. But this formula is acceptable because it's better to overestimate the amount of fuel needed rather than underestimate it.

If the turtle doesn't have enough fuel, the condition on line 86 returns `false` and line 87 terminates the program with the `error()` function and a message telling the player the turtle needs more fuel. Otherwise, if the condition on line 86 returns `true`, the turtle can begin farming by calling `hare.sweepField()` on line 92.

farmwheat

```
90.    -- farm wheat
91.    print('Sweeping field...')
92.    hare.sweepField(length, width, checkWheatCrop)
93.    storeWheat()
```

As in the previous chapters, the `hare.sweepField()` function takes the length and width of the field and controls the turtle's movements across the entire field. Line 92 passes `checkWheatCrop` to the `sweepField()` function. Remember not to enter `checkWheatCrop()` because if you add parentheses to the function name, Lua will call `checkWheatCrop()` and pass its return value to `hare.sweepField()` instead of passing the function.

The `hare.sweepField()` function returns after the turtle has harvested and planted the entire field. When the turtle is done sweeping, it needs to place the wheat it has in its inventory into the chest next to the starting space. We wrote the `storeWheat()` function to do this, which we call on line 93.

We want the turtle to plant and harvest continually, but the wheat that was just planted needs time to grow. If the turtle immediately starts sweeping the field again, none of the wheat will have time to grow and the turtle will waste fuel. Instead, we make the turtle pause for 10 minutes on line 95 and display a message to the player telling them this.

```
95.    print('Sleeping for 10 minutes...')
96.    os.sleep(600)
97. end
```

Line 96 calls os.sleep(), passing 600 to the function so the turtle pauses for 600 seconds (600 seconds divided by 60 seconds per minute equals 10 minutes). Line 97 ends the while loop that began on line 84.

BONUS ACTIVITY: GIANT WHEAT FIELDS

In this chapter, we've made the turtle farm a 9 x 9 area, but the farmwheat program can handle farms of any size. Create a giant wheat field like the one in Figure 14-1. Then run the program with command line arguments based on the size of your larger wheat field to make the turtle farm the entire area!

TIPS FOR AUTOMATING OTHER KINDS OF FARMING

Much of the code that runs in the farmwheat program is in hare.sweepField(). Because you can pass hare.sweepField() a function to call at each space in the field, it can accomplish a variety of tasks.

If you want to make other types of farms with ComputerCraft, you can write and pass functions that reuse the hare.sweepField() code to farm other crops. In the following sections, I provide some tips for writing different kinds of farming programs.

FARMING VEGETABLES

You can easily substitute vegetables for your wheat crops by changing a few values and names in your code. For example, checkWheatCrop() and plantWheatSeed() could be renamed checkVegCrop() and plantVeg(). Potatoes and carrots in Minecraft don't have seeds. Instead, you plant potato and carrot items directly into tilled soil using the turtle.placeDown() function, which produces multiple items when you harvest the mature plants. Figure 14-5 shows a turtle farming carrots.

You'll also need to replace the Minecraft name IDs the program checks for. For example, instead of calling hare.selectItem('minecraft:wheat_seeds'), your vegetable-farming program needs to call hare.selectItem('minecraft: potato') and hare.selectItem('minecraft:carrot').

Figure 14-5: A turtle programmed to farm carrots

Your vegetable-farming program shouldn't store all the carrots and potatoes it harvests in a chest, because it needs items to plant the next time the turtle sweeps the field.

MILKING COWS AND SHEARING SHEEP

Turtles can milk cows with an empty bucket or use shears to shear sheep for wool. You don't need to equip the turtle with these items. Instead, you put them in the turtle's currently selected slot. To provide enough space for the turtle to hover over the cows and sheep, the turtle must be two spaces above the ground (unlike one space for the other farms). Figure 14-6 shows the turtle hovering two spaces off the ground so it can sweep over cows and sheep.

Figure 14-6: Turtles must be two spaces off the ground to milk cows or shear sheep.

To milk a cow, the current slot must contain an empty bucket. While the turtle is above the cow, call the turtle.placeDown() function to fill the bucket with milk. To shear sheep, the current slot must have shears. While the turtle is above the sheep, call the turtle.placeDown() function to shear the sheep. The turtle automatically picks up any sheared wool.

The cows and sheep will move around the field, but you can use fences to contain them. It's possible they might evade the turtle as it sweeps across the field, but the turtle will find them more often than not. In addition, because cows and sheep are not blocks, calling turtle.inspectDown() won't work. Instead, the turtle will have to blindly call turtle.placeDown() with the empty bucket or shears in the current slot to milk or shear the livestock.

GATHERING CHICKEN EGGS

Chickens produce eggs every five to ten minutes, but like all dropped items, eggs will disappear after five minutes if they're not picked up. You can program turtles to sweep a field of chickens and pick the eggs off the ground.

To create a chicken farm, place chickens in a fenced-off rectangular field that the turtle sweeps. Then pass the turtle.suckDown function (without the parentheses) to the hare.sweepField() function to make the turtle pick up any items the chickens drop. Figure 14-7 features an egg-gathering turtle. Like livestock, eggs are not blocks, so turtle.inspectDown() won't identify them.

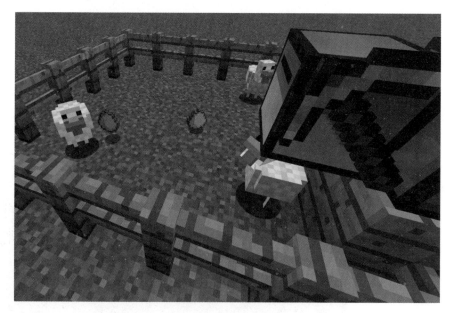

Figure 14-7: A turtle gathers eggs dropped by chickens.

FARMING CACTI AND SUGAR CANE

Cacti and sugar cane have specific growing requirements. For example, they both need at least a block of empty space separating them in order to grow, so you might need to adjust your code to skip rows to create a cacti or sugar cane farm.

Also, cacti can only grow on sand blocks, as shown in Figure 14-8.

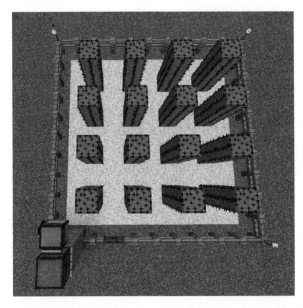

Figure 14-8: Cacti only grow on sand and must have a block of space separating them.

Sugar cane only grows on sand or dirt blocks that are adjacent to water, so every other row of your farm needs to be water blocks, as shown in Figure 14-9.

Figure 14-9: A turtle tends a sugar cane farm. Note that sugar cane must be planted next to water.

Both crops also grow up to three blocks in height. When a turtle hovers four blocks over a field of cacti or sugar cane, calling the turtle.digDown() function harvests any cactus or sugar cane that has grown to its maximum height. The Minecraft IDs for cactus and sugar cane are 'minecraft:cactus' and 'minecraft:reeds', respectively.

WHAT YOU LEARNED

By reusing the hare.sweepField() code, you can easily program turtles to automatically harvest several different kinds of crops. In this chapter, you learned how to use turtles to hoe dirt blocks, plant seeds, and detect mature wheat plants. Calling turtle.inspectDown() returns a table value that has a 'metadata' key whose value is a number from 0 to 7. When this number value is 7, the wheat is fully mature. The turtle uses this value to detect when the wheat is ready to be harvested with the diamond hoe.

The algorithm in hare.sweepField() has been useful for many different tasks. In Chapter 15, you'll develop a new algorithm for mining a stair-shaped hole into the earth.

15

PROGRAMMING A STAIRCASE MINER

From chopping trees and crafting stone bricks to farming wheat, turtles are now doing most of your chores for you. The last resources you need are those you mine from deep underground, such as iron, gold, diamond, coal, redstone, and lapis lazuli.

Your turtles can do this mining for you. Turtles come with a mining program named excavate, which you can use to mine a square hole straight down to the bedrock blocks at the bottom of the Minecraft world. However, as shown in Figure 15-1, you can easily fall into these deep holes, which makes them dangerous.

Figure 15-1: The excavate program creates deep, dangerous holes.

In this chapter, we'll write a mining program called stairminer that digs stairs into the earth, as shown in Figure 15-2. Near the surface, the turtle will mine mostly dirt and stone blocks. However, as it mines deeper, your turtle will find ore and diamond blocks.

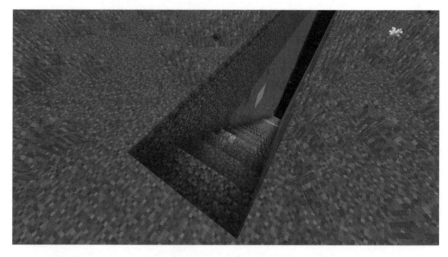

Figure 15-2: The stairminer program makes safe stairs while it mines.

After you've set up the stairminer program, you'll be able to mine ore without fear of falling into an abyss! These stairs also let you safely climb down into your mines so you can dig new tunnels or build an underground base.

DESIGNING THE STAIR-MINING ALGORITHM

Let's start by designing the stair-mining algorithm. Instead of just mining straight down to bedrock, the `stairminer` program cuts a stair-shaped pattern into the earth so your turtle won't make deadly holes you could fall into. The turtle starts on the surface, as shown in Figure 15-3.

Figure 15-3: The turtle on the surface, before mining

We want the algorithm to make the turtle dig a hole one space deep, then move one space forward, dig a hole two spaces deep, then move one space forward, dig a hole three spaces deep, and so on. The turtle should continue to dig until it reaches bedrock or a target depth the player specifies.

We'll need to translate this behavior into specific actions for the turtle to follow, and we'll also want to make sure the program is efficient. Every time the turtle mines down, it must return to the surface before digging down again. Because each move uses fuel, we want to limit the turtle's movement and ensure the turtle is digging as much as possible. We'll do this by programming the turtle not only to dig on its way down but also to dig on its way up. As a result, the turtle will use its fuel as efficiently as possible by mining columns every time it moves.

Let's look at the actions the stair-mining algorithm involves and figure out how we can minimize the amount of fuel the turtle uses at each part of the process.

As shown in Figure 15-4, the turtle mines the block at the X to create the first stair step in the algorithm's first part. Because the turtle doesn't move in this part, it doesn't use any fuel. The turtle only needs to dig the first stair step once at the beginning of the program, so the algorithm doesn't repeat this part.

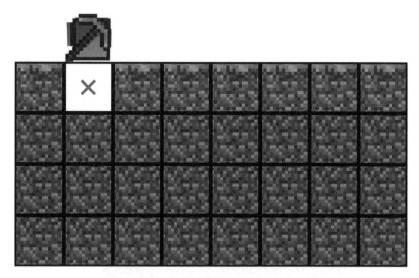

Figure 15-4: The turtle starts by digging below itself.

Next, the turtle moves forward one block to the next column it will mine, as shown in Figure 15-5. The turtle will repeat this action every time it starts a new column at the surface of the mine.

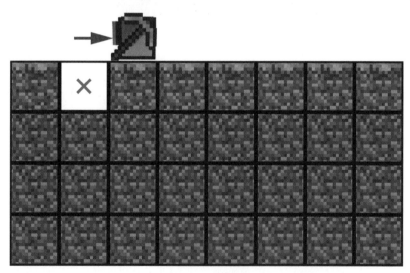

Figure 15-5: After digging the first column, the turtle moves forward one space to start the next column.

When the turtle is in position to mine the next column, it digs down one block more than it previously mined and moves into the empty space at the bottom of the column. Figure 15-6 shows this action.

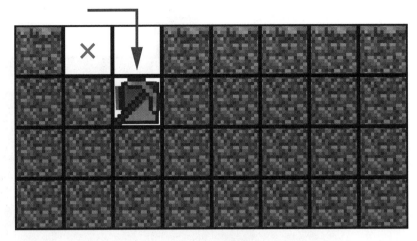

Figure 15-6: The turtle digs down from the surface for the next column.

After the turtle finishes mining down, it needs to mine the next column from the bottom up. The turtle mines the block in front of it and moves forward one space at the bottom of the column. When the turtle is in the next column, it needs to mine the block below it to make the column one block deeper than the previous column, as shown in Figure 15-7. Mining the two blocks doesn't use fuel, so the turtle uses only one unit of fuel in this action. The turtle repeats this action every time it starts a new column from inside the mine.

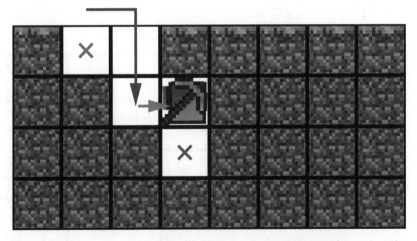

Figure 15-7: The turtle digs the block in front of it, moves one space forward, and then digs the block below it.

In the algorithm's last part, the turtle needs to mine up to complete the rest of the column. The turtle digs up to the surface, as shown by the orange arrow in Figure 15-8.

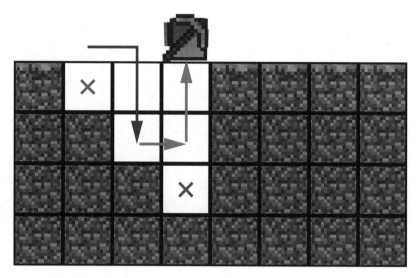

Figure 15-8: The turtle digs up, returning to the surface.

The turtle continues to repeat all the actions except the initial one where the turtle dug down one space at the first column. In other words, the turtle moves forward, digs down, starts a new column, and mines up, repeating the purple, green, and orange steps shown in Figure 15-9. The turtle repeats this mining pattern two columns at a time, mining down and then up. It continues until it reaches bedrock or the targeted depth.

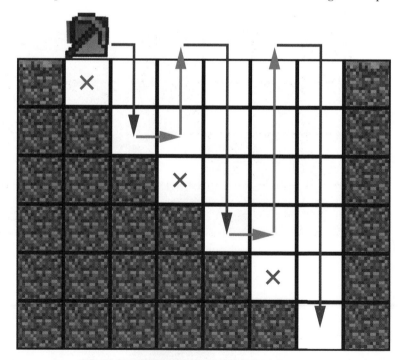

Figure 15-9: The stair pattern mined by the turtle

Before we can create the stairminer program, which uses the stair-mining algorithm we just outlined, we need to write some helper functions to handle situations where sand and gravel blocks might fall into the area the turtle is mining.

EXTENDING THE HARE MODULE

You might think that calling turtle.dig() always clears the space in front of a turtle, but it doesn't. If there are sand or gravel blocks above the block the turtle is digging, those blocks will fall down and block the turtle's path. Because the stair-mining algorithm we designed sometimes assumes the turtle has cleared a space in front of or above the turtle, you need a function that tells the turtle to keep digging until blocks stop falling into the space the turtle is trying to clear.

Figure 15-10 shows three sand blocks stacked on top of each other in front of the turtle. The turtle must call turtle .dig() three times to clear the sand.

To clear blocks, we'll write the digUntilClear() and digUpUntilClear() functions, which are nearly identical and clear blocks in front of the turtle and above the turtle, respectively. Because we can use these functions for many different turtle programs, we'll add them to the hare module. From the command shell, run **edit hare**. Move the cursor to the bottom of the file and continue the code by adding the following lines:

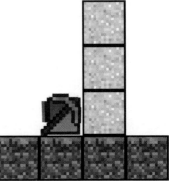

Figure 15-10: The turtle must dig three times to clear the space in front of it because the sand blocks will keep falling down.

hare

```
...snip...
216. -- digUntilClear() keeps digging until
217. -- there are no more blocks (used when
218. -- sand or gravel can fall into the path)
219. function digUntilClear()
220.   while turtle.detect() do
221.     if not turtle.dig() then
222.       return false
223.     end
224.   end
225.   return true
226. end
227.
228. -- digUpUntilClear() keeps digging up until
229. -- there are no more blocks (used when
230. -- sand or gravel can fall into the path)
231. function digUpUntilClear()
232.   while turtle.detectUp() do
```

```
233.    if not turtle.digUp() then
234.       return false
235.    end
236.  end
237.  return true
238. end
```

After entering these instructions, save the program and exit the editor. You can also download this program by running pastebin get wwzvaKuW hare.

WRITING THE DIGUNTILCLEAR() AND DIGUPUNTILCLEAR() FUNCTIONS

The digUntilClear() function repeatedly calls turtle.dig() until no blocks remain in front of the turtle. The function returns the value true if the space in front of the turtle is empty, and it returns false if the space can't be cleared (for example, if the turtle encounters unmineable bedrock blocks).

hare
```
216. -- digUntilClear() keeps digging until
217. -- there are no more blocks (used when
218. -- sand or gravel can fall into the path)
219. function digUntilClear()
220.    while turtle.detect() do
221.      if not turtle.dig() then
222.         return false
223.      end
224.    end
225.    return true
226. end
```

The function needs to continue calling turtle.dig() as long as there is a block in front of the turtle, so on line 220 the function uses a while loop to instruct the turtle to dig indefinitely. This loop keeps looping as long as turtle.detect() returns true, which indicates the turtle detects a block in front of it.

Line 221 calls turtle.dig(), which returns false if the turtle can't dig the block in front of it. The turtle.dig() function returns false for two reasons: when there is an empty space with nothing to dig or when there is a bedrock block that can't be mined. The execution doesn't enter the while loop if an empty space is detected because turtle.detect() would have returned false, making not turtle.detect() a true condition. This means that when turtle.dig() returns false in the while loop, the turtle must be facing a bedrock block. In that case, the turtle can't possibly clear the block in front of it.

Otherwise, the loop keeps looping as long as a block is in front of the turtle. Once the space is clear, the execution exits the loop at line 224. Line 225 returns true from the function.

The digUpUntilClear() function's code on lines 228 to 238 is almost identical to digUntilClear() except it calls turtle.detectUp() instead of turtle.detect() and turtle.digUp() instead of turtle.dig().

With our helper functions in place to make the stair-mining algorithm possible, let's write the stairminer program!

WRITING THE STAIRMINER PROGRAM

The stairminer program mines a stair-shaped pattern into the ground in front of the turtle. From the command shell, run **edit stairminer** and enter the following code:

stairminer

```
1. --[[Stair Miner program by Al Sweigart
2. Mines in a stair pattern.]]
3.
4. os.loadAPI('hare')
5.
6. local cliArgs, targetDepth, columnDepth, result, errorMessage
7.
8. cliArgs = {...}
9. targetDepth = tonumber(cliArgs[1])
10.
11. -- display "usage" info
12. if targetDepth == nil or cliArgs[1] == '?' then
13.   print('Usage: stairminer <depth>')
14.   return
15. end
16.
17. turtle.digDown()
18.
19. columnDepth = 2
20. while true do
21.   -- move forward
22.   hare.digUntilClear()
23.   turtle.forward()
24.
25.   -- mine while descending
26.   for i = 1, columnDepth do
27.     -- check for bedrock
28.     result, errorMessage = turtle.digDown()
29.     if errorMessage == 'Unbreakable block detected' then
30.       print('Hit bedrock. Done.')
31.       return
32.     else
33.       turtle.down()
34.     end
35.   end
36.
37.   -- check if done
38.   print('Current depth: ' .. columnDepth)
39.   if columnDepth >= targetDepth then
40.     print('Done.')
41.     return
42.   end
43.
```

```
44.    -- move forward
45.    hare.digUntilClear()
46.    turtle.forward()
47.    turtle.digDown()
48.
49.    -- check if there's enough fuel to go up and back down again
50.    while turtle.getFuelLevel() < (columnDepth * 2) do
51.      -- try to burn fuel items in the inventory
52.      for slot = 1, 16 do
53.        turtle.select(slot)
54.        turtle.refuel()
55.      end
56.
57.      if turtle.getFuelLevel() < (columnDepth * 2) then
58.        print('Please load more fuel...')
59.        os.sleep(10)
60.      end
61.    end
62.
63.    -- check for a full inventory
64.    while hare.selectEmptySlot() == false do
65.      print('Please unload the inventory...')
66.      os.sleep(10)
67.    end
68.
69.    -- mine while ascending
70.    for i = 1, columnDepth do
71.      hare.digUpUntilClear()
72.      turtle.up()
73.    end
74.
75.    columnDepth = columnDepth + 2
76.  end
```

After you've entered all of these instructions, save the program and exit the editor.

RUNNING THE STAIRMINER PROGRAM

Set the turtle on the ground, and then run the stairminer program by passing an integer argument for the target depth. For example, stairminer 6 will make the turtle mine a stair-shaped path six blocks deep. Note that the stairminer program rounds up to the nearest even number because it will always move down one column and then move up the next column. So, stairminer 9 will mine a stair-shaped path 10 blocks deep, the same as if stairminer 10 had been run.

If you get errors when running this program, carefully compare your code to the code in this book to find any typos. If you still cannot fix your program, delete the file by running delete stairminer and then download it by running pastebin get PGH1WYpH stairminer.

SETUP FOR THE STAIRMINER PROGRAM

The first four lines of stairminer consist of comments describing the program and a call to os.loadAPI() to load the hare module. After the program is set up, we declare several variables we'll use in the program.

stairminer

```
6. local cliArgs, targetDepth, columnDepth, result, errorMessage
```

Line 6 uses a local statement to create five variables. The cliArgs variable contains the command line arguments the program uses when it executes. The targetDepth and columnDepth variables keep track of how far down the turtle should go and how far the turtle has gone up or down a column, respectively. The result and errorMessage variables store the return values from turtle.digDown() calls.

Next, the program stores the command line argument in the targetDepth variable. If the player didn't enter a number for the command line argument or they entered '?', the program displays a usage message.

stairminer

```
8. cliArgs = {...}
9. targetDepth = tonumber(cliArgs[1])
10.
11. -- display "usage" info
12. if targetDepth == nil or cliArgs[1] == '?' then
13.    print('Usage: stairminer <depth>')
14.    return
15. end
```

The command line arguments are stored in the {...} table, which line 8 stores in a variable named cliArgs. When the player doesn't enter a number for the command line argument (for example, if the player runs stairminer hello), the tonumber(cliArgs[1]) expression on line 9 evaluates to nil, which sets targetDepth to nil. Line 12 checks if the value in targetDepth is nil or if the command line argument is '?'. If either condition on line 12 is true, the code on lines 13 and 14 runs and shows the program's usage message.

CREATING THE FIRST STAIR STEP

Recall that the turtle doesn't have to move down to dig the first column. The turtle starts at the surface, digs down, and then moves forward to the next column. Line 17 tells the turtle to dig downward, creating a one-block-deep column. This action makes the first step in the stair-shaped path.

stairminer

```
17. turtle.digDown()
```

The first column only needs to be dug once, so the stair-mining algorithm never repeats this first action. The turtle digs the rest of the columns using a while loop and alternates between digging down and digging up. The turtle digs down for the first two columns, and then it digs up for the third column. After the first three columns, the turtle digs down for every even column and up for every odd column. Let's look at the code that tells the turtle to dig the even columns.

MINING DOWNWARD

The `columnDepth` variable stores the number of blocks the turtle should dig for the column it's currently mining.

stairminer

```
19. columnDepth = 2
20. while true do
21.     -- move forward
22.     hare.digUntilClear()
23.     turtle.forward()
```

Because the turtle digs the first column before the loop, `columnDepth` starts at 2 and increases at the end of each iteration of the `while` loop that begins on line 20. Inside the `while` loop, line 22 clears the block in front of the turtle by using `hare.digUntilClear()`. If sand or gravel blocks keep falling in front of the turtle, `hare.digUntilClear()` ensures that all the blocks are cleared before line 23 tells the turtle to move forward one space. When the program finishes line 23, the turtle is in position to dig the rest of the next column.

After the turtle has moved forward, we create a for loop to run in the `while` loop.

stairminer

```
25.     -- mine while descending
26.     for i = 1, columnDepth do
27.       -- check for bedrock
28.       result, errorMessage = turtle.digDown()
29.       if errorMessage == 'Unbreakable block detected' then
30.         print('Hit bedrock. Done.')
31.         return
32.       else
33.         turtle.down()
34.       end
35.     end
```

The for loop on line 26 tells the turtle to dig downward by calling `turtle.digDown()` on line 28. However, the digging could fail if the turtle is at the bottom of the Minecraft world, where there are unbreakable bedrock blocks. On line 28, if bedrock is below the turtle, `turtle.digDown()` returns false for its first return value (which we store in the result variable) and the string `'Unbreakable block detected'` for its second return value (which we store in errorMessage). Line 29 checks for the `'Unbreakable block detected'` string in errorMessage, and if the string is there, line 30 displays the message Hit bedrock. Done. to the player. When the turtle hits bedrock, it can't continue to dig the stairs, so the program terminates on line 31.

Otherwise, if no bedrock is detected below the turtle, the turtle can move down and the program continues to the else statement on line 32. Line 33 is inside the else statement's block and moves the turtle down into the dug-out space. Line 34 ends the else statement's block, and line 35 ends the for loop's block. The code inside the for loop from lines 26 to 35 makes the turtle dig down columnDepth times (or until the turtle reaches bedrock).

After digging the column and exiting the for loop, the program runs through the rest of the while loop.

stairminer

```
37.   -- check if done
38.   print('Current depth: ' .. columnDepth)
39.   if columnDepth >= targetDepth then
40.     print('Done.')
41.     return
42.   end
```

Line 38 prints columnDepth, which is the number of spaces down the turtle moved in the for loop on lines 26 to 35. The if statement on line 39 checks whether columnDepth (the depth of the column the turtle will dig) is equal to or greater than the targetDepth. If the condition is true, line 40 tells the player the program is done, and the return statement on line 41 terminates the program. Remember: A return statement outside of all functions, like the one on line 41, will terminate a ComputerCraft program.

If the turtle hasn't reached bedrock after digging down a column, the turtle should clear the space in front of it, move forward, and dig down once. These actions create a stair below the turtle for the next column.

stairminer

```
44.   -- move forward
45.   hare.digUntilClear()
46.   turtle.forward()
47.   turtle.digDown()
```

On line 45, the turtle calls hare .digUntilClear() to dig the block in front of it. Line 46 moves the turtle forward by calling turtle.forward(). Line 47 digs the block that's now below the turtle by calling turtle .digDown(). Figure 15-11 shows the state of the stair pattern being carved by the turtle after line 47 executes. The turtle will then mine the column it is currently in from the bottom up.

But before the turtle can mine upward, we need the turtle to check whether it has enough fuel to continue the stair-mining process. Let's look at how that fuel check works.

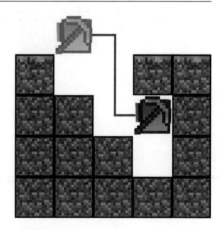

Figure 15-11: The stair mine after line 47 executes

CHECKING THE TURTLE'S FUEL

When the turtle mines down the even columns, you can easily follow it down the stairs and retrieve the turtle if it runs out of fuel. But if the turtle runs out of fuel as it's mining up the odd columns, it might be floating too far above your head to reach it. For example, you don't want the turtle to run out of fuel when it is halfway up a tall column, like the one shown in Figure 15-12.

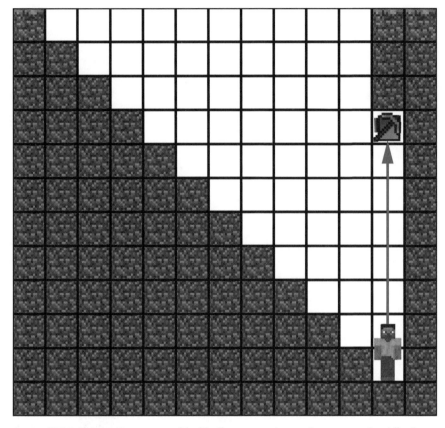

Figure 15-12: If the turtle runs out of fuel halfway up a deep column, it can be difficult to reach.

The turtle needs to check that it has enough fuel to reach the surface and then go back down. Because the for loop on lines 26 to 35 makes the turtle move down columnDepth number of times, the turtle also needs to move up columnDepth number of times to complete a column up to the surface. This means the turtle must move columnDepth * 2 to go down the current column and back up to the surface again. (Recall that the turtle only uses one unit of fuel per movement. Digging and turning don't use fuel.)

If the turtle doesn't have at least columnDepth * 2 units of fuel, it should start consuming any fuel items it has in its inventory. As the turtle carves out the stair-shaped mine, it often mines coal or other blocks it can use as fuel. When the turtle runs low on fuel, we can have the turtle use the mined coal in its inventory to power itself up. The while loop that begins on line 50 checks the turtle's fuel level by calling getFuelLevel().

stairminer

```
49.   -- check if there's enough fuel to go up and back down again
50.   while turtle.getFuelLevel() < (columnDepth * 2) do
```

If the turtle has less fuel than columnDepth * 2, the execution enters the while loop's block and begins searching for fuel in the turtle's inventory.

A for loop inside the while loop searches for fuel in each of the turtle's inventory slots.

stairminer

```
51.   -- try to burn fuel items in the inventory
52.   for slot = 1, 16 do
53.     turtle.select(slot)
54.     turtle.refuel()
55.   end
```

The for loop on line 52 makes the slot variable iterate over the numbers 1 to 16. On each iteration of the for loop, line 53 selects slot number slot in the turtle's inventory and line 54 attempts to have the turtle consume the items in the slot as fuel. If the items aren't usable as fuel, the turtle.refuel() function does nothing.

After consuming any fuel in its inventory, the turtle rechecks whether it has less than columnDepth * 2 fuel. If it still needs more fuel, the turtle prints the message Please load more fuel... and waits 10 seconds for the player to manually put fuel items into its inventory.

stairminer

```
57.   if turtle.getFuelLevel() < (columnDepth * 2) then
58.     print('Please load more fuel...')
59.     os.sleep(10)
60.   end
61. end
```

Line 57 checks the turtle's fuel level using the same condition that appeared in the while statement on line 50. If the turtle consumed more than columnDepth * 2 units of fuel, the program skips the if statement's block. When the if statement's block is skipped, the execution reaches the end of the while loop on line 61 and goes back to line 50 to recheck the while loop's condition. The while loop on line 50 uses the same condition as the if statement on line 77, so the condition on line 50 will also be false. This is how the execution moves past the while loop when the turtle has enough fuel.

However, if the condition on line 57 is true because the turtle doesn't have enough fuel, line 58 displays the message Please load more fuel... to the player and then pauses for 10 seconds by calling os.sleep(10) on line 59. After the pause, the execution reaches the end of the while loop and goes back to line 50 to recheck the condition.

If the player has put more fuel items in the turtle's inventory, those items are consumed on the next iteration of the while loop. If the player hasn't added items to the turtle's inventory, the turtle's fuel level stays the same, and the program goes through the while loop again. When the while loop runs again, the program displays the message Please load more fuel... and waits another 10 seconds. Until the player puts enough fuel in the turtle's inventory to make getFuelLevel() return a number larger than columnDepth * 2, the turtle continues waiting for fuel.

After the program ensures that the turtle has enough fuel, it needs to check to make sure the turtle's inventory isn't full before it can begin digging up the next column. Let's look at how this check works next.

CHECKING THE TURTLE'S INVENTORY

If the turtle passes its fuel check, the execution leaves the while loop and is ready to perform its inventory check. The turtle drops any mined blocks if its inventory is already full, which is a waste of blocks. The turtle should check whether it has a full inventory while it is at the bottom of a column so that if it's full, the player can reach the turtle to unload it.

The selectEmptySlot() function in the hare module selects the first empty slot it finds in the turtle's inventory. However, we don't need to select an empty inventory slot for stair mining. Because the selectEmptySlot() function returns false if there are no empty inventory slots, we can use it to determine if the turtle's inventory is full.

stairminer
```
63.    -- check for a full inventory
64.    while hare.selectEmptySlot() == false do
65.       print('Please unload the inventory...')
66.       os.sleep(10)
67.    end
```

The while loop on line 64 uses selectEmptySlot() to check whether the inventory has at least one empty slot. If the turtle doesn't have an empty slot, the execution enters the while loop's block, line 65 displays a Please unload the inventory... message, and line 66 waits 10 seconds. This code is similar to what lines 58 and 59 did for the fuel check. The while loop only stops looping after the player unloads the turtle's inventory and selectEmptySlot() returns true. After the inventory check, the program continues to line 70 and the turtle mines upward back to the surface.

MINING UPWARD

Because the turtle is columnDepth spaces beneath the surface, it needs to mine columnDepth blocks up to return to the surface. The for loop on line 70 causes the turtle to dig and move upward.

stairminer
```
69.    -- mine while ascending
70.    for i = 1, columnDepth do
71.       hare.digUpUntilClear()
72.       turtle.up()
73.    end
```

Line 71 calls digUpUntilClear() before moving up. We use the function hare.digUpUntilClear() instead of turtle.digUp() when digging up because sand or gravel could be above the turtle. When the loop ends, the turtle will be back at the surface.

Line 75 increments columnDepth by 2 because the loop makes the turtle mine two columns at a time, and so we need to increase columnDepth by two blocks at each iteration.

stairminer

```
75.  columnDepth = columnDepth + 2
76. end
```

By increasing columnDepth by 2, the turtle moves two units deeper the next time it digs downward. Line 76 is the end statement for the while loop on line 20. When the execution loops back to line 20, lines 22 and 23 will move the turtle forward over the next space, where it will continue to mine down and then back up to the surface. The turtle only stops when columnDepth is equal to or greater than targetDepth (which the player supplied as a command line argument) or when the turtle hits bedrock.

After running the stairminer program, you'll have a stair-shaped hole that gives you safe access deep underground, and your inventory will contain all the blocks the turtle mined while making it.

BONUS ACTIVITY: TALL TUNNEL

You might want to start a tunnel at the bottom of the stairs your turtle constructs. Turtles come with a program called tunnel that will dig a 3 × 2 hole in front of the turtle with a length specified through a command line argument. For example, you can run tunnel 10 and the turtle will dig a 3 × 2 × 10 tunnel. These tunnels are just tall enough for the player to walk through, but they can feel claustrophobic. Try creating your own talltunnel program that does what the tunnel program does but creates tunnels four blocks high.

WHAT YOU LEARNED

The stairminer program uses a complex algorithm, but once you write it, you can leave the drudgery of mining to your turtles. Even if you don't need the blocks that the stairminer program mines, you could use this program to carve out the staircases for a subterranean lair with stone brick walls (crafted from your cobblestone generator) lining the sides. As long as you can program instructions for the turtle, the possibilities are endless!

By learning how to code and speaking the computer's language, you can get an army of turtles to automate many tasks in Minecraft. Programming is a useful and fun skill, and I hope you'll continue to experiment more on your own. When it comes to programming, there's always more to learn, so get going and invent your own turtle programs. Good luck!

FUNCTION REFERENCE

In this reference, you'll find short descriptions of every function used in this book. The functions are grouped by application programming interface (API), also known as a module. This reference is not a complete list of all the functions in ComputerCraft, but you can read about other available functions in the documentation that ComputerCraft provides at *http://computercraft.info/ wiki/Category:APIs*.

If you want to learn more about Lua, you can use the Lua 5.1 Reference Manual, which is available online at *https://www.lua.org/manual/5.1/*. Note that ComputerCraft uses Lua 5.1, even though newer versions of Lua are available.

FS (FILE SYSTEM) API

Turtles and in-game Minecraft computers have file systems similar to those your computer has. You can interact with these files using the fs API and the file's name:

fs.delete(*string filename*)   Deletes a file named *filename*

fs.exists(*string filename*)   Returns true if a file named *filename* exists; otherwise returns false

NOTE   *The programs you write in this book can interact with the files loaded on a turtle or in-game computer but not with the files on the computer that is running Minecraft.*

HARE API

You wrote the hare API while reading this book. Unlike the other APIs listed in this reference, hare doesn't come with ComputerCraft, so you must first run pastebin get wwzvaKuW hare from the CLI shell to download it. Each program you write that uses the hare API must include the code os.loadAPI('hare') in order for the program to call the hare module's functions:

hare.buildFloor(*number length, number width*)   Builds a floor *length* blocks long and *width* blocks wide using items in the turtle's inventory.

hare.buildRoom(*number length, number width, number height*)   Builds a room *length* blocks long, *width* blocks wide, and *height* blocks tall using items in the turtle's inventory.

hare.buildWall(*number length, number height*)   Builds a wall *length* blocks long and *height* blocks tall using items in the turtle's inventory.

hare.countInventory()   Returns the total number of items in all the turtle's inventory slots.

hare.digUntilClear()   Continues to mine the space in front of the turtle until the space contains no blocks. You use this function when gravel or sand could fall in front of the turtle as it mines the block in front of it.

hare.digUpUntilClear()   Similar to hare.digUntilClear() except it clears the space *above* the turtle.

hare.findBlock(*string name*)   Spins the turtle around and stops if the turtle is facing a block named *name*. If the turtle can't find the block, the turtle ends up facing its original direction after the function code finishes running. Returns true if the block was found; otherwise returns false.

hare.selectAndPlaceDown()   Selects a nonempty inventory slot and places the item in that slot beneath the turtle.

hare.selectEmptySlot() Selects an empty inventory slot. Returns true if a slot is found; otherwise returns false.

hare.selectItem(*string name*) Selects an inventory slot containing an item named *name*. Returns true if the item is found; otherwise returns false.

hare.sweepField(*number length, number width, function sweepFunc*) Moves the turtle over every space in a rectangular field *length* blocks long and *width* blocks wide, calling *sweepFunc* at each space.

IO (INPUT/OUTPUT) API

When you use the io API, programs can display text on the screen and also accept text from the player via the keyboard. There are several functions in the io API, but the most important function to know is io.read():

io.read() When the player types a response and presses ENTER, this function returns the response as a string value.

MATH API

The math API is part of Lua, and you can call its functions from non-ComputerCraft Lua programs. This API includes the following number and mathematics-related functions:

math.ceil(*number num*) Returns *num* rounded up.

math.floor(*number num*) Returns *num* rounded down.

math.random(*number start, number end*) Returns a random whole number between *start* and *end*, including *start* and *end*. The *start* and *end* arguments are optional. If no arguments are passed, the function returns a decimal point number between 0.0 and 1.0. If the *start* argument is not used, the function returns an integer between 1 and *end*.

OS (OPERATING SYSTEM) API

The ComputerCraft operating system provides the following functions, which are useable by turtles and in-game computers:

os.getComputerLabel() Returns a string of the turtle's label (that is, its name).

os.loadAPI(*string filename*) Loads the program named *filename* as a module so the current program can call its functions.

os.setComputerLabel(*string/nil label*) Sets the turtle's label to *label*. If *label* is nil, the function erases the turtle's label.

os.sleep(*number time*) Pauses the program for *time* number of seconds.

SHELL API

Turtles can run commands from the CLI the same way the player can run commands from the CLI. You can run a CLI command in a turtle program using the shell API:

shell.run(*string command*)   Runs *command* as though the player entered the string at the CLI shell. Returns false if the *command* terminates because the command doesn't exist, crashes, or calls error(); otherwise returns true.

STRING API

The string API is part of Lua, and you can call its functions from non-ComputerCraft Lua programs. Although these functions weren't featured in this book, I've included them here because they're useful:

string.find(*string haystack, string needle*)   Looks for the *needle* string inside the *haystack* string and returns two integers: the position where the *needle* string was found and where this string ends. For example, string.find('hello', 'el') returns 2 and 3, because 'el' is found at the second character in 'hello' and ends at the third character. If the *needle* string is not in the *haystack* string, the function returns nil. The *needle* string can also find text patterns, which are outside the scope of this book. You can learn more about text patterns at *https://www.lua.org/manual/5.1/manual.html#5.4.1/*.

string.sub(*string bigstring, number start, number length*)   Returns a substring, or portion, of *bigstring*, starting at the *start* position and returning the next *length* characters. The *length* argument is optional. If *length* is not passed, the substring starts at start and continues to the end of *bigstring*. For example, string.sub('hello', 3, 2) returns 'll' and string.sub('hello', 2) returns 'ello'.

TEXTUTILS API

Using textutils, you can make programs display text one character at a time to create a fancy typewriter effect:

textutils.slowPrint(*string text, number rate*)   Similar to print() except it writes the characters in *text* one character at a time. The *rate* argument is optional and specifies how many characters are printed per second.

TURTLE API

The turtle API holds all the common functions that your programs could call to make a turtle perform some action. Let's look at these functions in batches based on the actions the functions can trigger.

BUILDING FUNCTIONS

You can call functions to make turtles build by placing blocks. But the same function can also cause the turtle to perform other actions, depending on the item in the turtle's current slot:

turtle.place() Performs an action with the item in the turtle's current slot. For building blocks, this function places the block in the Minecraft world. However, if one of the special items listed in Table 1 is in the current slot, that item will be used in the way specified by Table 1. The function returns false if the turtle is unable to place the block or perform an action on the block.

turtle.placeDown() Similar to turtle.place() but performs the action on the space below the turtle.

turtle.placeUp() Similar to turtle.place() but performs the action on the space above the turtle.

Table 1: Special Items That the place Functions Can Use

Item	Action
Armor	Sets the armor on an armor stand.
Boats	Places the boat on water.
Dyes	Dyes a sheep.
Empty bucket	Collects lava or water. Can also collect milk from a cow.
Fireworks	Launches the fireworks.
Flint and steel	Sets fire to a flammable block or activates a Nether portal.
Minecarts	Places the minecart on tracks.
Saplings, flowers, or seeds	Plants the object in a dirt or grass block.
Shears	Shears a sheep and collects its wool.
Sign	Places a sign with text on it. To write text on the sign, pass the turtle function a string. For example, turtle.place('This\nis a\nsign.').
Spawn eggs	Spawns a mob.

FUELING FUNCTIONS

Turtles use one unit of fuel each time they move, but they can't move if they run out of fuel. For this reason, refueling the turtle and understanding its fueling functions are important:

turtle.getFuelLevel() Returns the amount of fuel the turtle currently has stored. Returns 'unlimited' if the *ComputerCraft.cfg* config file has disabled the fuel requirement.

turtle.getFuelLimit() Returns the maximum amount of fuel the turtle can store. For most turtles, the limit is 20,000 units; for other types of turtles, the limit is 100,000 units. Returns 'unlimited' if the *ComputerCraft.cfg* config file has disabled the fuel requirements.

turtle.refuel(*number amount*) Consumes *amount* of fuel items in the current slot. The *amount* argument is optional. If *amount* is not given, the function consumes all the items in the current slot by default.

INVENTORY FUNCTIONS

Each turtle has an inventory with 16 numbered slots. You can use various inventory functions to make the turtle perform actions on its inventory. These functions often take a number to indicate which of the numbered slots to perform an action on.

turtle.compareTo(*number slot*) Returns true if the item in the current slot is the same as the item in *slot*; otherwise returns false.

turtle.drop(*number amount*) Drops *amount* items from the current slot into the space or container in front of the turtle. The *amount* argument is optional. If *amount* isn't given, the function drops all the items in the current slot. Returns true if any items were dropped; otherwise returns false.

turtle.dropDown(*number amount*) Similar to turtle.drop() except this function drops items into the space or container *below* the turtle.

turtle.dropUp(*number amount*) Similar to turtle.drop() except this function drops items into the space or container *above* the turtle.

turtle.equipLeft() Unequips the tool, if any, on the turtle's left side and equips the tool in the current slot. Returns true if equipped; otherwise returns false.

turtle.equipRight() Unequips the tool, if any, on the turtle's right side and equips the tool in the current slot. Returns true if equipped; otherwise returns false.

turtle.getItemCount(*number slot*) Returns the number of items in *slot*. Uses the current slot if *slot* isn't given.

turtle.getItemDetail(*number slot*) Returns a table value of information about the item in *slot* or returns nil if the slot is empty. Uses the current slot if *slot* isn't given.

turtle.getItemSpace(*number slot*) Returns the amount of free space in *slot*. Uses the current slot if *slot* isn't given.

turtle.getSelectedSlot() Returns the slot number (1 to 16) of the current slot.

turtle.select(*number slot*) Changes the current slot to *slot*, a number from 1 to 16.

turtle.suck(*number amount*) Takes *amount* items from the space or container in front of the turtle, sucking them up like a vacuum cleaner, and places them in either the current slot (if empty) or the first available empty slot. The *amount* argument is optional. If *amount* isn't given, a full stack of items is taken. (A full stack is 64 for most items, although some items like eggs, snowballs, or empty buckets can only stack up to 16.) Returns true if any items were taken; otherwise returns false.

turtle.suckDown(*number amount*)   Like turtle.suck() except this function takes items from the space or container *below* the turtle.

turtle.suckUp(*number amount*)   Like turtle.suck() except this function takes items from the space or container *above* the turtle.

turtle.transferTo(*number slot, number amount*)   Transfers *amount* items from the current slot to *slot*. The *amount* argument is optional. If *amount* isn't given, the function attempts to transfer all items in the current slot to *slot*. Returns true if any items were transferred; otherwise returns false.

MOVEMENT FUNCTIONS

Turtles can move in any direction as long as the space they're attempting to move to is not already occupied by another block. You can use the following functions to tell a turtle to move in various directions. All movement functions return true if the turtle was able to move; otherwise, they return false:

turtle.back()   Moves the turtle backward one space

turtle.down()   Moves the turtle down one space

turtle.forward()   Moves the turtle forward one space

turtle.turnLeft()   Turns the turtle to the left; doesn't use fuel

turtle.turnRight()   Turns the turtle to the right; doesn't use fuel

turtle.up()   Moves the turtle up one space

PERCEPTION FUNCTIONS

Turtles can examine blocks one space in front of, above, or below them using the following functions:

turtle.compare()   Returns true if the block in front of the turtle is of the same type as the block in the current slot; otherwise returns false.

turtle.compareDown()   Similar to turtle.compare() but compares the block *below* the turtle to the item in the current slot.

turtle.compareUp()   Similar to turtle.compare() but compares the block *above* the turtle to the item in the current slot.

turtle.detect()   Returns true if a block is in front of the turtle; otherwise returns false.

turtle.detectDown()   Similar to turtle.detect() but checks the block *below* the turtle.

turtle.detectUp()   Similar to turtle.detect() but checks the block *above* the turtle.

turtle.inspect()   Returns two values: true and a table value with information about the block in front of the turtle. If no block is in front of the turtle, returns false.

turtle.inspectDown()   Similar to turtle.inspect() but returns information about the block *below* the turtle.

turtle.inspectUp()   Similar to turtle.inspect() but returns information about the block *above* the turtle.

TOOL-RELATED FUNCTIONS

Turtles can perform actions with the tools they have equipped, and there are corresponding tool-related functions for each action the turtle can perform. You can equip turtles with diamond pickaxes, shovels, axes, swords, hoes, and crafting benches to make the following functions available:

turtle.attack()   If equipped with a sword, the turtle attacks anything in front of the turtle. Returns true if a mob was attacked; otherwise returns false if nothing was attacked.

turtle.attackDown()   Similar to turtle.attack() but the turtle attacks the space *below* it.

turtle.attackUp()   Similar to turtle.attack() but the turtle attacks the space *above* it.

turtle.craft(*number amount*)   When you lay out items for a recipe in the turtle's inventory, this function crafts *amount* number of items and puts them in the current slot. Requires the turtle to equip a crafting table. The *amount* argument is optional. If *amount* isn't given, the function will craft as many items as possible. Returns true if something was crafted; otherwise returns false when no recipe matches the laid-out items.

turtle.dig()   Mines or tills the block in front of the turtle. The turtle must be equipped with a pickaxe for this function to mine blocks. If the turtle has equipped a hoe, the function tills the block in front of the turtle. Returns true if something was mined or hoed; otherwise returns false.

turtle.digDown()   Similar to turtle.dig() but mines or tills the block *below* the turtle.

turtle.digUp()   Similar to turtle.dig() but mines the block *above* the turtle. Note that this function cannot till dirt blocks.

LUA FUNCTIONS

The following functions come with the Lua language, so you don't need to type a module name before the function name when calling these functions:

error(*string message*)   Terminates the program and displays *message*, if given. The *message* argument is optional.

exit()   Exits the interactive shell. You can use this only while in the interactive shell.

print(*string/number value*)   Displays *value* on the screen, followed by a newline. The *value* argument is optional. If no *value* is passed, the function only displays a newline.

NAME ID REFERENCE

 In this book, you used the name IDs of Minecraft blocks to write your programs. This reference lists the block name IDs so you can reference them when modifying the programs you wrote in this book or when writing new programs on your own. Before looking at the list of IDs, let's review how to find a block's name ID.

FINDING A BLOCK'S NAME ID

You need to know a block's name ID when you're working with specific types of blocks in your programs. When your turtle is facing a block, as shown in Figure 1, use the turtle.inspect() function to determine what type of block is in front of the turtle.

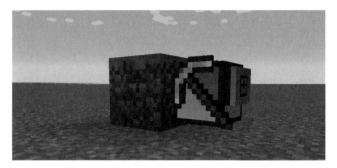

Figure 1: A turtle facing a grass block before calling turtle.inspect()

You can find all the information associated with a block by calling turtle.inspect() and examining the table value the function returns. The 'name' key in the returned table contains the name ID of the block in front of the turtle. For example, if the turtle is in front of a grass block and you call turtle.inspect() in the Lua shell, the returned table should look like the following:

```
lua> turtle.inspect()
true
{
  state = {
    snowy = false,
  },
  name = "minecraft:grass",
  metadata = 0,
}
```

The grass block's name ID is "minecraft:grass". In most cases, the name ID will be enough to identify the blocks you want to use in your programs. But in some cases, you might need to also use other keys in the table that turtle.inspect() returns.

DISTINGUISHING BETWEEN BLOCKS THAT SHARE NAME IDS

Some blocks share name IDs, and you can only uniquely identify them from other keys in the table. For example, oak wood planks and spruce wood planks have the same name ID of "minecraft:planks", but their metadata keys have different values. If you call turtle.inspect() when the turtle is in front of oak wood planks, the function returns the following table:

```
lua> turtle.inspect()
true
{
  state = {
    variant = "oak",
  },
  name = "minecraft:planks",
```

```
    metadata = 0,
}
```

But if the turtle is in front of spruce wood planks, the function returns this table:

```
lua> turtle.inspect()
true
{
  state = {
    variant = "spruce",
  },
  name = "minecraft:planks",
  metadata = 1,
}
```

Although the name ID of both blocks is "minecraft:planks", you can use the different metadata values (0 for oak and 1 for spruce) to distinguish between the two block types in your programs. These plank blocks also have a state key containing a table with a variant key that holds more information about the block.

LIST OF BLOCK NAME IDS

Table 1 lists the name IDs for most of the blocks your turtle might interact with. However, Table 1 doesn't distinguish between blocks that share name IDs. For example, the table lists the name ID of wood planks but doesn't list the keys that distinguish between oak wood planks and spruce wood planks. In situations where you want to distinguish between blocks that share name IDs, you'll need to use turtle.inspect() to find out which values in the tables are different for the blocks.

Table 1: Minecraft Name IDs

Icon	Name	Name ID	Icon	Name	Name ID
	Acacia Door	'minecraft:acacia_door'	None	Air	'minecraft:air'
	Acacia Fence	'minecraft:acacia_fence'		Anvil	'minecraft:anvil'
	Acacia Fence Gate	'minecraft:acacia_fence _gate'		Beacon	'minecraft:beacon'
	Acacia Wood Stairs	'minecraft:acacia_stairs'		Bed	'minecraft:bed'
	Activator Rail	'minecraft:activator_rail'		Bedrock	'minecraft:bedrock'

Icon	Name	Name ID	Icon	Name	Name ID
	Beetroots	'minecraft:beetroots'		Brown Shulker Box	'minecraft:brown_shulker _box'
	Birch Door	'minecraft:birch_door'		Cactus	'minecraft:cactus'
	Birch Fence	'minecraft:birch_fence'		Cake	'minecraft:cake'
	Birch Fence Gate	'minecraft:birch_fence _gate'		Carpet	'minecraft:carpet'
	Birch Wood Stairs	'minecraft:birch_stairs'		Carrots	'minecraft:carrots'
	Black Glazed Terracotta	'minecraft:black_glazed _terracotta'		Cauldron	'minecraft:cauldron'
	Black Shulker Box	'minecraft:black_shulker _box'		Chest	'minecraft:chest'
	Blue Glazed Terracotta	'minecraft:blue_glazed _terracotta'		Chorus Flower	'minecraft:chorus_flower'
	Blue Shulker Box	'minecraft:blue_shulker _box'		Chorus Plant	'minecraft:chorus_plant'
	Bone Block	'minecraft:bone_block'		Clay	'minecraft:clay'
	Bookshelf	'minecraft:bookshelf'		Coal Block	'minecraft:coal_block'
	Brewing Stand	'minecraft:brewing_stand'		Coal Ore	'minecraft:coal_ore'
	Brick Stairs	'minecraft:brick_stairs'		Cobblestone	'minecraft:cobblestone'
	Bricks	'minecraft:brick_block'		Cobblestone Stairs	'minecraft:stone_stairs'
	Brown Glazed Terracotta	'minecraft:brown_glazed _terracotta'		Cobblestone Wall	'minecraft:cobblestone _wall'
	Brown Mushroom	'minecraft:brown_mushroom'		Cobweb	'minecraft:web'
	Brown Mushroom Block	'minecraft:brown _mushroom_block'		Cocoa	'minecraft:cocoa'

Icon	Name	Name ID	Icon	Name	Name ID
	Concrete	`'minecraft:concrete'`		Double Red Sandstone Slab	`'minecraft:double_stone _slab2'`
	Concrete Powder	`'minecraft:concrete_powder'`		Double Stone Slab	`'minecraft:double_stone _slab'`
	Crafting Table	`'minecraft:crafting_table'`		Double Wooden Slab	`'minecraft:double_wooden _slab'`
	Cyan Glazed Terracotta	`'minecraft:cyan_glazed _terracotta'`		Dragon Egg	`'minecraft:dragon_egg'`
	Cyan Shulker Box	`'minecraft:cyan_shulker _box'`		Dropper	`'minecraft:dropper'`
	Dandelion	`'minecraft:yellow_flower'`		Emerald Block	`'minecraft:emerald_block'`
	Dark Oak Door	`'minecraft:dark_oak_door'`		Emerald Ore	`'minecraft:emerald_ore'`
	Dark Oak Fence	`'minecraft:dark_oak_fence'`		Enchantment Table	`'minecraft:enchanting _table'`
	Dark Oak Fence Gate	`'minecraft:dark_oak_fence _gate'`		End Gateway	`'minecraft:end_gateway'`
	Dark Oak Wood Stairs	`'minecraft:dark_oak_stairs'`		End Portal	`'minecraft:end_portal'`
	Daylight Sensor	`'minecraft:daylight _detector'`		End Portal Frame	`'minecraft:end_portal _frame'`
	Dead Bush	`'minecraft:deadbush'`		End Rod	`'minecraft:end_rod'`
	Detector Rail	`'minecraft:detector_rail'`		End Stone	`'minecraft:end_stone'`
	Diamond Block	`'minecraft:diamond_block'`		End Stone Bricks	`'minecraft:end_bricks'`
	Diamond Ore	`'minecraft:diamond_ore'`		Ender Chest	`'minecraft:ender_chest'`
	Dirt	`'minecraft:dirt'`		Farmland	`'minecraft:farmland'`
	Dispenser	`'minecraft:dispenser'`		Fence Gate	`'minecraft:fence_gate'`

Icon	Name	Name ID	Icon	Name	Name ID
	Fire	`'minecraft:fire'`		Gray Shulker Box	`'minecraft:gray_shulker _box'`
	Flower Pot	`'minecraft:flower_pot'`		Green Glazed Terracotta	`'minecraft:green_glazed _terracotta'`
	Flowing Lava	`'minecraft:flowing_lava'`		Green Shulker Box	`'minecraft:green_shulker _box'`
	Flowing Water	`'minecraft:flowing_water'`		Hardened Clay	`'minecraft:hardened_clay'`
	Frosted Ice	`'minecraft:frosted_ice'`		Hay Bale	`'minecraft:hay_block'`
	Furnace	`'minecraft:furnace'`		Hopper	`'minecraft:hopper'`
	Glass	`'minecraft:glass'`		Ice	`'minecraft:ice'`
	Glass Pane	`'minecraft:glass_pane'`		Inverted Daylight Sensor	`'minecraft:daylight _detector_inverted'`
	Glowing Redstone Ore	`'minecraft:lit_redstone _ore'`		Iron Bars	`'minecraft:iron_bars'`
	Glowstone	`'minecraft:glowstone'`		Iron Block	`'minecraft:iron_block'`
	Gold Block	`'minecraft:gold_block'`		Iron Door	`'minecraft:iron_door'`
	Gold Ore	`'minecraft:gold_ore'`		Iron Ore	`'minecraft:iron_ore'`
	Grass	`'minecraft:grass'`		Iron Trapdoor	`'minecraft:iron_trapdoor'`
	Grass Path	`'minecraft:grass_path'`		Jack o' Lantern	`'minecraft:lit_pumpkin'`
	Grass (Tall)	`'minecraft:tallgrass'`		Jukebox	`'minecraft:jukebox'`
	Gravel	`'minecraft:gravel'`		Jungle Door	`'minecraft:jungle_door'`
	Gray Glazed Terracotta	`'minecraft:gray_glazed _terracotta'`		Jungle Fence	`'minecraft:jungle_fence'`

Icon	Name	Name ID	Icon	Name	Name ID
	Jungle Fence Gate	`'minecraft:jungle_fence_gate'`		Magenta Glazed Terracotta	`'minecraft:magenta_glazed_terracotta'`
	Jungle Wood Stairs	`'minecraft:jungle_stairs'`		Magenta Shulker Box	`'minecraft:magenta_shulker_box'`
	Ladder	`'minecraft:ladder'`		Magma Block	`'minecraft:magma'`
	Lapis Lazuli Block	`'minecraft:lapis_block'`		Melon	`'minecraft:melon_block'`
	Lapis Lazuli Ore	`'minecraft:lapis_ore'`		Melon Stem	`'minecraft:melon_stem'`
	Large Flowers	`'minecraft:double_plant'`		Mob Head	`'minecraft:skull'`
	Leaves	`'minecraft:leaves'`		Mob Spawner	`'minecraft:mob_spawner'`
	Leaves (Acacia/Dark Oak)	`'minecraft:leaves2'`		Monster Egg	`'minecraft:monster_egg'`
	Lever	`'minecraft:lever'`		Moss Stone	`'minecraft:mossy_cobblestone'`
	Light Blue Glazed Terracotta	`'minecraft:light_blue_glazed_terracotta'`		Mycelium	`'minecraft:mycelium'`
	Light Blue Shulker Box	`'minecraft:light_blue_shulker_box'`		Nether Brick	`'minecraft:nether_brick'`
	Light Gray Glazed Terracotta	`'minecraft:silver_glazed_terracotta'`		Nether Brick Fence	`'minecraft:nether_brick_fence'`
	Light Gray Shulker Box	`'minecraft:silver_shulker_box'`		Nether Brick Stairs	`'minecraft:nether_brick_stairs'`
	Lily Pad	`'minecraft:waterlily'`		Nether Portal	`'minecraft:portal'`
	Lime Glazed Terracotta	`'minecraft:lime_glazed_terracotta'`		Nether Quartz Ore	`'minecraft:quartz_ore'`
	Lime Shulker Box	`'minecraft:lime_shulker_box'`		Nether Wart	`'minecraft:nether_wart'`
	Lit Furnace	`'minecraft:lit_furnace'`		Nether Wart Block	`'minecraft:nether_wart_block'`

Icon	Name	Name ID	Icon	Name	Name ID
	Netherrack	'minecraft:netherrack'		Prismarine	'minecraft:prismarine'
	Note Block	'minecraft:noteblock'		Pumpkin	'minecraft:pumpkin'
	Oak Door	'minecraft:wooden_door'		Pumpkin Stem	'minecraft:pumpkin_stem'
	Oak Fence	'minecraft:fence'		Purple Glazed Terracotta	'minecraft:purple_glazed _terracotta'
	Oak Wood Stairs	'minecraft:oak_stairs'		Purple Shulker Box	'minecraft:purple_shulker _box'
	Observer	'minecraft:observer'		Purpur Block	'minecraft:purpur_block'
	Obsidian	'minecraft:obsidian'		Purpur Double Slab	'minecraft:purpur_double _slab'
	Orange Glazed Terracotta	'minecraft:orange_glazed _terracotta'		Purpur Pillar	'minecraft:purpur_pillar'
	Orange Shulker Box	'minecraft:orange_shulker _box'		Purpur Slab	'minecraft:purpur_slab'
	Packed Ice	'minecraft:packed_ice'		Purpur Stairs	'minecraft:purpur_stairs'
	Pink Glazed Terracotta	'minecraft:pink_glazed _terracotta'		Quartz Block	'minecraft:quartz_block'
	Pink Shulker Box	'minecraft:pink_shulker _box'		Quartz Stairs	'minecraft:quartz_stairs'
	Piston	'minecraft:piston'		Rail	'minecraft:rail'
	Piston Head	'minecraft:piston_head'		Red Glazed Terracotta	'minecraft:red_glazed _terracotta'
	Poppy	'minecraft:red_flower'		Red Mushroom	'minecraft:red_mushroom'
	Potatoes	'minecraft:potatoes'		Red Mushroom Block	'minecraft:red_mushroom _block'
	Powered Rail	'minecraft:golden_rail'		Red Nether Brick	'minecraft:red_nether _brick'

Icon	Name	Name ID	Icon	Name	Name ID
	Red Sandstone	'minecraft:red_sandstone'		Sandstone Stairs	'minecraft:sandstone_stairs'
	Red Sandstone Slab	'minecraft:stone_slab2'		Sapling	'minecraft:sapling'
	Red Sandstone Stairs	'minecraft:red_sandstone_stairs'		Sea Lantern	'minecraft:sea_lantern'
	Red Shulker Box	'minecraft:red_shulker_box'		Slime Block	'minecraft:slime'
	Redstone Block	'minecraft:redstone_block'		Snow	'minecraft:snow'
	Redstone Comparator (Powered)	'minecraft:powered_comparator'		Snow Layer	'minecraft:snow_layer'
	Redstone Comparator (Unpowered)	'minecraft:unpowered_comparator'		Soul Sand	'minecraft:soul_sand'
	Redstone Lamp (Active)	'minecraft:lit_redstone_lamp'		Sponge	'minecraft:sponge'
	Redstone Lamp (Inactive)	'minecraft:redstone_lamp'		Spruce Door	'minecraft:spruce_door'
	Redstone Ore	'minecraft:redstone_ore'		Spruce Fence	'minecraft:spruce_fence'
	Redstone Repeater (Active)	'minecraft:powered_repeater'		Spruce Fence Gate	'minecraft:spruce_fence_gate'
	Redstone Repeater (Inactive)	'minecraft:unpowered_repeater'		Spruce Wood Stairs	'minecraft:spruce_stairs'
	Redstone Torch (Active)	'minecraft:redstone_torch'		Stained Clay	'minecraft:stained_hardened_clay'
	Redstone Torch (Inactive)	'minecraft:unlit_redstone_torch'		Stained Glass	'minecraft:stained_glass'
	Redstone Wire	'minecraft:redstone_wire'		Stained Glass Pane	'minecraft:stained_glass_pane'
	Sand	'minecraft:sand'		Standing Banner	'minecraft:standing_banner'
	Sandstone	'minecraft:sandstone'		Standing Sign	'minecraft:standing_sign'

Icon	Name	Name ID	Icon	Name	Name ID
	Stationary Lava	`'minecraft:lava'`		Wall Banner	`'minecraft:wall_banner'`
	Stationary Water	`'minecraft:water'`		Wall Sign	`'minecraft:wall_sign'`
	Sticky Piston	`'minecraft:sticky_piston'`		Weighted Pressure Plate (Heavy)	`'minecraft:heavy_weighted_pressure_plate'`
	Stone	`'minecraft:stone'`		Weighted Pressure Plate (Light)	`'minecraft:light_weighted_pressure_plate'`
	Stone Brick Stairs	`'minecraft:stone_brick_stairs'`		Wheat	`'minecraft:wheat'`
	Stone Bricks	`'minecraft:stonebrick'`		White Glazed Terracotta	`'minecraft:white_glazed_terracotta'`
	Stone Button	`'minecraft:stone_button'`		White Shulker Box	`'minecraft:white_shulker_box'`
	Stone Pressure Plate	`'minecraft:stone_pressure_plate'`		Wood	`'minecraft:log'`
	Stone Slab	`'minecraft:stone_slab'`		Wood (Acacia/Dark Oak)	`'minecraft:log2'`
	Sugar Cane	`'minecraft:reeds'`		Wood Planks	`'minecraft:planks'`
	TNT	`'minecraft:tnt'`		Wooden Button	`'minecraft:wooden_button'`
	Torch	`'minecraft:torch'`		Wooden Pressure Plate	`'minecraft:wooden_pressure_plate'`
	Trapdoor	`'minecraft:trapdoor'`		Wooden Slab	`'minecraft:wooden_slab'`
	Trapped Chest	`'minecraft:trapped_chest'`		Wool	`'minecraft:wool'`
	Tripwire	`'minecraft:tripwire'`		Yellow Glazed Terracotta	`'minecraft:yellow_glazed_terracotta'`
	Tripwire Hook	`'minecraft:tripwire_hook'`		Yellow Shulker Box	`'minecraft:yellow_shulker_box'`
	Vines	`'minecraft:vine'`			

INDEX

refuel() function, 205, 214
refuel program, 13, 15–16
Render Distance option,
        Minecraft, 90
return statement, 74
return value, 18, 74
rom folder, 30
room-building algorithm, 144–145
running programs, 29–30

S

sand blocks, 189, 197, 202
saplings, planting, 86, 91–92
saving programs, 28–29
sayhello program, 73
scope
    global, 81–82
    local, 81–82
select() function, 79, 116, 122, 214
selectAndPlaceDown() function,
        130–131, 155, 156, 210
selectEmptySlot() function, 78, 211
selectItem() function, 76, 78–79,
        170, 186, 211
setComputerLabel() function,
        33–34, 211
sheep, shearing, 187–188
shell
    command, 12, 13
    Lua, 17–19
shell.run() function, 70, 94, 212
single quote ('), 31
sleep() function, 96, 105, 110, 122,
        186, 211
slots (inventory), 13, 78. *See also*
        current slot
slowPrint() function, 33, 212
Sofonisba, 13, 29, 32
source code, 28
spruce tree, 89
stack (inventory), 13
stairminer program, 199–200
stair-mining algorithm, 193–197
step number, 41
sticks, 14
stone bricks, 121–122

strings
    concatenation operator (..),
        31–32
    data type, 31
    empty, 31
string.find() function, 212
string.sub() function, 212
subtraction operator (-), 20
suck() function, 120, 214
suckDown() function, 120, 188, 215
suckUp() function, 120, 215
sugar cane, farming, 189–190
survival mode, 6–7, 11, 127, 173
sweeping algorithm, 154–158
sweepField() function, 161–163,
        185, 211
sweepFunc parameter, 154–155

T

table data type, 80, 93
text editor, 5
    running programs in, 29–30
    saving programs in, 28–29
textutils.slowPrint() function,
        33, 212
then keyword, 52
toggling, 136, 163, 170
tonumber() function, 139, 180, 201
tools
    diamond, 12, 60
    wooden, 14
transferTo() function, 121, 215
tree-chopping algorithm, 61–62
tree-farming algorithm, 86
tree types, 89
true value, 18, 50, 51
turtleappstore.com, 44
turtle.attack() function, 216
turtle.attackDown() function, 216
turtle.attackUp() function, 216
turtle.back() function, 37–39, 215
turtle.compare() function, 69, 215
turtle.compareDown() function, 69, 215
turtle.compareTo() function, 214
turtle.compareUp() function, 69, 215
turtle.craft() function, 116, 121, 216

RESOURCES

Visit the book's web page at *https://www.nostarch.com/codingwithminecraft/* for updates and resources. You can import the programs in this book from *https://pastebin.com/* directly to your turtle by following the instructions in "Sharing and Downloading Programs Online" on page 42. You can also find the programs from this book and programs other users have created at *https://turtleappstore.com/*. This book's programs are also available for download from the book's web page.

REQUIREMENTS

Here's what you'll need in order to follow along with this book! The software you need to install is the same whether you use Windows, macOS, or Linux:

- The official, paid version of Minecraft, available from *https://minecraft.net/*

- Java, available for free from *http://www.java.com/en/download/*

- The ATLauncher software, available for free from *https://www.atlauncher.com/*

- The ComputerCraft mod, available for free from *http://www.computercraft.info/*

See Chapter 1 for detailed installation instructions.

You'll also need a desktop or laptop computer with Windows 7 or later or macOS 10.10 or later to follow along with this book. The ComputerCraft mod isn't compatible with Minecraft Pocket Edition or Minecraft Raspberry Pi Edition.